In the Beginning

The Truth Behind Genesis

In the Beginning

The Truth Behind Genesis

by
Robert R. Davis

In the Beginning
© Copyright 2013, Robert R. Davis

All rights reserved. No part of this book may be reproduced, stored in a retrieval system, or transmitted by any means, electronic, mechanical, photocopying, recording, or otherwise – except for brief quotations in printed reviews, without written permission from the author.

All scripture quotations, unless otherwise indicated, are taken from the Holy Bible (King James Version) 1.42.01. Copyright © 1992-2004 by Timnathserah Inc. Used by permission of Online Bible, www.OnlineBible.org. All rights reserved. The author has inserted italics and bolding used in quotations from Scripture.

Table of Contents

Prologue 7

The Story of Creation 19

The Story of Creation (Alternate Version) 49

The Garden of Eden 79

The Fall of Mankind 109

The Serpent Revisited 139

Out of Eden 149

Prologue

The Bible is first foremost a spiritual book. Its intent is to define the purpose and relationship between God and humanity. In doing so, it defines our relationship to all of creation, including each other. Explaining the origins of the universe is not the intent of the Bible, but it does give us a brief overview from a spiritual vantage point. Therefore, the Genesis creation narrative may not be as clear-cut as it appears. This will become apparent when we look at the story of Adam and Eve.

"The Old Testament scribes were not concerned with factual information about bygone events, but with their religious significance. In Scripture God's pleasure or displeasure with something is the focal point, not historical meticulousness. Victory or defeat in war, peace or social unrest, abundance of harvest or famine, only serves to demonstrate the virtue or sinfulness of the nation [Israel] and to forecast its future destiny."[1]

One of the main features of the Bible is its declaration that it is the Word of Truth. If this is the case, time should reveal the validity of the claims in scripture. Science and Religion have been at odds for centuries, but in my opinion, this should not be the case. If the Bible is stating fundamental truths, then science should be able to corroborate at least some of its claims.

> **Science** - knowledge or a system of knowledge covering general truths or the operation of general

laws especially as obtained and tested through scientific method.[2]

What does this really mean? Science refers to a system of acquiring knowledge. This system explains natural phenomena based on observation and experimentation. As science exposes to us the how's and why's of things that are recorded in the Bible, the mystical should give way to the practical and we should begin to see the Truths of God, more clearly.

Genesis 1:1 In the beginning God created the heaven and the earth.
Genesis 1:2 And the earth was without form, and void; and darkness was upon the face of the deep. And the Spirit of God moved upon the face of the waters.

Unfortunately, science cannot confirm everything in the Bible. Genesis chapter one, verse one states, "In the beginning God created the heavens and the earth." This first statement in the Bible tells us two things immediately. First, God created our universe. Second, it does not explain His origins. It is not the intent of Genesis or the Bible to explain the Creator. We do however derive from the very first sentence God is outside of time. Since, our concept of time begins with the creation of the universe. Without matter, we cannot measure time.

Since the Bible contends, God created all matter. He is outside of time. Science will never prove the existence of God. Why is this, the case? In order for science to prove God exists. He must first, be observable. Then we need to test, what we observed.

St. John 1:18 ***No man hath seen God at any time****; the only begotten Son, which is in the bosom of the Father, he hath declared him.*

Exodus 33:20 And he said, Thou canst not see my face: for ***there shall no man see me, and live.***

The book of St. John declares no one has ever been able to observe God. The book of Exodus takes it one step further and states, "No one can see God and live." This does not mean if we could see Him, that our heads would explode. I believe the writer is expressing that our current human form is not compatible with God's composition. It also seems to imply after this life, we will be able to see Him. However, after death, we might obtain full knowledge of God and yet He could remain invisible to us. We may find the Lord to be comprehensible, but eternally imperceptible.

1 Corinthians 13:12 ***For now we see through a glass, darkly; but then face to face:*** *now I know in part; but then shall I know even as also I am known.*

I know Paul said we would see Him, face to face. However, the Bible uses the same language concerning Moses. The book of Exodus states, "The Lord spoke to Moses face to face, as a man speaks to his friend." (Exodus 33:11) This of course was poetic language, meant to convey the relationship not the physical encounter between them. Moses never saw God's face.

We cannot see God. This does not indicate He is not real. Oxygen under normal circumstances is invisible, but it is certainly real. In modern times, we have found ways to test for the presence of it. Even though today we understand the properties of air, we still cannot see it. It may be the same with God.

The Bible proclaims in the beginning God made the heavens and the earth. The writer is stating creation is not an accident or happenstance. He declares it was the intent of the Lord to create the world. This statement seems to be in direct opposition to science.

Stephen Hawking in his book the *Grand Design* states, "It is reasonable to ask who or what created the universe, but if the answer is God, then the question has merely been deflected to that of who created God."[3] This assertion is not entirely true. For instance, if you see your friend with a beautifully carved chair and you ask, "Who made it?" If he responds, Robert made it. Just because you do not know who I am, does not mean I did not make the chair? Does it mean your friend deviated from the question? The answer is no, of course not.

The real problem science has with God being the creator of the universe is the fact that it cannot define God. Therefore, the Genesis's claim of God creating the heavens and earth may be valid, but it is frustrating from a scientific standpoint.

So how do we know God created the universe? The quick answer is because the Bible says He did. The underlying assumption is the Bible is the unerring Word of God. Faith then is the criteria and justification for everything the scriptures express. "Faith is not blind trust. Unfounded belief is foolishness. Faith is rooted and grounded in the truth of God's Word, not man, not Church doctrine or theology."[4] So, if biblical faith is not blind, what is it?

> *Hebrews 11:1 Now faith is **the substance** of things hoped for, **the evidence** of things not seen.*

Hebrews states faith is both substance and evidence. Substance means material. It is normally something tangible or concrete. Faith is also evidence. Evidence is the proof, sign, or substantiation of something. Based on Hebrews faith is the following:

- The tangible material of things hoped for
- The proof of things not seen

The proof and tangible material referred to here is not scientific proof, but rather the type of proof used in a court of law. Courts use the law of evidence, as proof. The most common form of evidence used in courtrooms throughout history, are the testimonies of witnesses. We cannot use the rules and standards of courts today when viewing scriptures. We must use the standards of their day in order to see what constitutes proof. Fortunately, we do not have to research history to obtain the norm. The Bible gives us the gauge.

> *Deuteronomy 19:15 One witness shall not rise up against a man for any iniquity, or for any sin, in any sin that he sinneth:* **at the mouth of two witnesses, or at the mouth of three witnesses, shall the matter be established.**

So, in order for our faith to be based in truth and not merely having blind faith, we must have two or three witnesses. When we talk about faith, understand it is not static, but a growing, steady process within a person. First, we will look at the evidence of faith and then the substance of it.

The evidence of faith is the Word of God. How can scripture serve as a witness? The sixty-six books of the Bible represent various authors' testimonies of God stretching across two different ages. Therefore, in order to establish biblical evidence we need agreement from two or three different sources. I personally think the best criteria would be to find two or three scriptures written by different authors. The harmony or agreement of the witnesses is the foundation for faith.

In a court of law after hearing all of the evidence, either the judge or the jury must make a ruling. All rulings from courts are subjective, because they are the judgments of someone. Likewise, when viewing the Word, the person reviewing the scriptures must make a judgment. Consequently, faith is subjective proof.

This brings us to our next component of proof, the substance of faith. Tangible faith is an oxymoron. In what way is faith tangible? First, based on the evidence of faith (the scriptures), a person must make a judgment as to what they believe. Then, if you believe the Word is true, you must follow with some sort of action. Otherwise, as the apostle James says, "Faith without works is dead [useless]."[5]

"True faith has three components, belief, words and actions."[6] Faith works by what we think, say and do. Prayer must also have these elements in order to be effective. Belief springs from the Word of God, also known as our evidence. Our words are not just our prayers, but also our inner dialogue. They must be in agreement with our beliefs, in order to achieve any results. Likewise, our actions must agree with our words or our faith will be void. When all three agree, there will be an answer to our prayer. That is not my opinion. It is what the Bible declares.

The question still remains, how can faith serve as proof? Answered prayer is the substance or tangible evidence of our faith. Again, this proof is not objective, but subjective. In order to get an answer we must first believe. In order to believe, we must make a judgment about the Word of God. Consequently, if you judge the scriptures false, then you will not believe. If you do not believe, then you will not pray and if you do not pray, then you will never have tangible proof of God. This is why the Bible says, if we seek God with all our heart and soul [mind] we will find Him."[7]

Back to original question, how do we know God created the universe? We know because of the witnesses of scripture and the substance of our answered prayers. In other words, we have confirmed it through our faith. We are confident because of our faith. We believe the whole Word of God, is true. This type of confidence in the Word builds progressively.

Psalms 119:160 declares, "God's Word is true from the beginning and endures forever." From a biblical standpoint the witness of scriptures and the proof of answered prayers validates the Bible is true, in its entirety. Therefore, faith is not the ignorant beliefs of foolish people. Faith consists of biblical proof and deductive reasoning. True faith requires logic, not blind acceptance.

1. The Word of God is true (major premise)
2. Answered prayer is proof of its correctness (minor premise)
3. Therefore, answered prayer proves the Word is true, progressively (conclusion)

The first premise is absolute truth. The second premise is subjective proof, but it substantiates the first. So, the test of the major premise depends solely on the minor. Meaning the personal subjective proof (small scale), gives us confidence in the correctness of the absolute truth of God's Word (large scale). This is the model of faith.

The truth is the truth, whether we believe it or not. Faith does not alter facts. However, believing does affect what we perceive to be true. This does not mean it is all in our heads. Quantum Theory (Physics) states, "The act of watching directly affects the observed reality. In fact, experiments have shown, the greater the amount of watching, the more the observer influences what actually takes place."[8] This is exactly how an individual's belief or faith affects their prayers. To boil it down, our perception (belief) becomes our reality (subjective truth).

Science for the most part discounts the Bible. Consequently, their theories eliminate the stipulation for a God. The book, *The Great Design* makes the conclusion, "Because there is a law like gravity, the universe can and will create itself from nothing. Spontaneous creation is the reason there is something rather than nothing, why the universe exists, why we exist. It is not necessary to invoke god to light the blue touch paper and set the universe going." [9]

I am neither a scientist nor a theologian, so I will try to tread lightly here. Nevertheless, spontaneous creation fails to explain why the laws like gravity would be in place prior to creation.

> **Gravity** - a fundamental physical force that is responsible for interactions which occur because of mass between particles, between aggregations of matter (as stars and planets), and between particles (as photons) and aggregations of matter, that is 10^{-39} times the strength of the strong force, and that extends over infinite distances but is dominant over

macroscopic distances especially between aggregations of matter.

In others words, gravity causes objects to move towards each other. However, if there were no objects (matter), why would the law of gravity exist? The Bible states, something from nothing is how God made the earth. Science has come to the same conclusion.

Hebrews 11:3 ***Through faith we understand that the worlds*** *were framed by the word of God, so that things* ***which are seen were not made of things which do appear.***

Paul states the invisible made the visible. The apostle reveals God is the invisible instigator of the cosmos. Science describes it as spontaneous creation. Paul proclaims faith gives us this understanding. This tells us why science comes to one conclusion and religion another. The observers are affecting their own outcomes.

Whether you believe God created the universe or it formed spontaneously. Both views claim something emerged from nothing. I believe in this instance we could paraphrase Shakespeare and call it, "A rose by any other name."

If through faith we believe God exists, then we can confidently go forward and study how He created the universe. We should never study the Bible in a vacuum, but in light of life itself. Therefore, since creation is a natural phenomenon, we should look at it in conjunction with science not apart from it. Einstein had this to say about it, "Science without religion is lame. Religion without science is blind." I would have to concur with him on this point. Therefore, this book will attempt to look at the Bible with the eyes of faith and compare it to what science has discovered.

In Genesis 1:2, at the start of creation there was only darkness. Connected to this declaration is a curious occurrence, the Spirit of God was hovering over the waters. The waters referred to here are not oceans or seas, but space. In ancient times and even today, space is likened to water. Notice, in verses six through eight the sky (expanse) separated the water under and over it. There is no actual water over the sky, only space, which is deep, dark and mysterious like the seas. The question before us is, why is the Spirit hovering over space or darkness?

In order to understand this image we must look at the tabernacle or temple of God. The tabernacle is composed of three parts, the Outer Court, the Inner Court and the Holiest of Holies. The Outer Court receives light from the sun. The Inner Court receives light from the candlesticks or lampstands. The Holiest of Holies never receives light, natural or manufactured. This is the dwelling place of the Spirit and it is always dark.

So, what is the meaning of the Spirit hovering over the darkness of space? The Spirit of God hovers over the mercy seat in the tabernacle and rules Israel. God is symbolically declaring before there was anything, I existed and was sovereign.

Why does the Lord need to make this statement? Remember, the book of Genesis originated after Israel's exodus from Egypt. God needs to undo four hundred years of polytheism. Therefore, He declares, I am God and there is no other.[10] This is the first statement of Genesis and from there He begins creation.

Before we delve into the days of creation, it is important to note God hides spiritual truths throughout His Word. Consequently, we must always pray for the Holy Spirit to reveal the meaning of scriptures, even the seemingly straightforward ones.

The Golden Rule of Interpretation
When the plain sense of scripture makes common sense, seek no other sense; *therefore, take every word at its primary, ordinary, usual, literal meaning unless the facts of the immediate context, studied in the light of related passages and axiomatic and fundamental truths, indicate clearly otherwise.*

Rules of interpretation are needful when trying to understand any biblical text. However, we must recognize the golden rule of interpretation will only give us the most rudimentary understanding. Knowing scriptures have dual meanings, cryptic images, hidden implications, we cannot always adhere to the "seek no other sense" clause.

Proverbs 25:2 ***It is the glory of God to conceal a thing****: but the honour of kings is to search out a matter.*

This why we must we must cry out for knowledge, lift up our voices for understanding, seek wisdom like silver and search for it like hidden treasures (Proverbs 2:3-4). We can never stop seeking other meanings from the Bible, since it is the distinguished quality (glory) of God to conceal things in His Word.

This means the story of creation may not be as literal or straightforward as we originally thought. This is important to keep in mind, when we look at Genesis chapters two and three.

The next chapter will look at creation narrative given in Genesis 1. Since the Bible uses the law of evidence as proof, I will describe the story of creation in two different formats. The first will be in the normal narrative form and the second is to be read as a courtroom proceeding. It is not necessary to read both. The bulk of the information is in each account. So, choose which version you want to read and skip the other.

The Story of Creation

Day 1

Genesis 1:3 And God said, Let there be light: and there was light.
Genesis 1:4 And God saw the light, that it was good: and God divided the light from the darkness.
Genesis 1:5 And God called the light Day, and the darkness he called Night. And the evening and the morning were the first day.

The first action of God is the creation of light. He says, "Let there be light." Consequently light appeared. The point the writer is trying to convey is God spoke and it happened. How can God just speak something into existence? He does so in accordance with the law of faith.

> *Romans 3:27 Where is boasting then? It is excluded. By what law? of works? Nay: but by **the law of faith**.*

Faith has three components, belief (what we think), words (what we say) and actions (what we do). God operates according to faith. Why would God need faith?

Faith is a law. It is not something reserved for religious people. It is how we create what we need and want in this life. Nothing created in this universe came into being without this law.

Therefore, we have the ability to create, just like God. In fact, we do it all the time. How did we build the first airplane? It all started with an idea (thought or belief in the mind). Once someone believed they could fly, they began to align their words with their actions. Their contemporaries probably said, "If God meant for us to fly, He would have given us wings." The Creator gave us something better than wings. He gave us the law of faith.

Not only do we see God in the first chapter of Genesis creating the world. He is also laying down a pattern for us to mimic.

The Bible claims light was God's first creation, is this true? Remember, the Bible uses the type of proof used in a court of law and not scientific proof. Does this mean we exclude science, not at all? How does science fit in to the courtroom scheme? Science will be our expert witness and their findings will serve as evidence.

According to science, what happened in the beginning? "The Big Bang Model is a broadly accepted theory for the origin and evolution of our universe. It postulates 12 to 14 billion years ago, that the portion of the universe we can see today was only a few millimeters across. It has since expanded from this hot dense state into the vast and much cooler cosmos we currently inhabit."[11]

In an attempt to corroborate this theory, NASA sent a probe into space. The Wilkinson Microwave Anisotropy Probe (WMAP) launched in June 2001 to make fundamental measurements of cosmology -- the study of the properties of our universe as a whole.

"WMAP found that the universe is 13.7 billion years old. The universe began with an unimaginably enormous density and temperature. This immense primordial energy was the cauldron from whence all life arose. There was matter and antimatter. When they met, they annihilated each other and created light. Somehow, it seems there was a tiny fraction more matter than antimatter, so when nature took its course, the universe was left with some matter, very little antimatter, and a tremendous amount of light."[12]

Science and the scriptures agree the first thing created in our universe was light. Since this is an agreement of two or more sources (Big Bang Theory, NASA and Genesis), we can confidently say, this is true.

Although the first thing created was light, it was not the light of the sun. The first light came from the radiation emitted by the Big Bang and later stars formed. The sun, which is also a star, did not form for almost 8 billion years after the bang.

No wonder Paul calls Him the God of patience.[13] I would have gone for the quick method.

Currently, there is some debate in the scientific community as to what was before the Big Bang. Some say nothing existed and others insist something must have been there prior to the event. The Bible does not clearly tell us. It just states, "Darkness was upon the face of the deep and the Spirit of God moved upon the face of the waters." We will have to wait on science to find out what, if anything existed before our current universe.

In Day 1 the scriptures states, God divided the light from the darkness. Darkness is simply the absence or relative absence of light. Therefore, God would not have to separate light from darkness, when He created light, darkness would naturally vanish. Another peculiar thing to note is the statement, "God called the light Day, and the darkness He called Night."

So, what is really happening here? Well, we know from science the universe started by combining matter and antimatter, the Big Bang. It is plausible the writer is describing the separation of matter from antimatter or dark matter.

"Modern theories of particle physics and of the evolution of the universe suggest, or even require, that antimatter and matter were equally common in the earliest stages of time. So why is antimatter so uncommon today? The observed imbalance between matter and antimatter is a puzzle still requiring explanation. Without it, the universe today would certainly be a much less interesting place, because there would be essentially no matter left around; annihilations would have converted everything into electromagnetic radiation by now. So clearly, this imbalance is a key property of the world we know. Attempts to explain it are an active area of research today."

We know why God would separate matter from antimatter. If He did not, there would be cosmic explosions, sporadically happening all over the universe. We are still looking for our expert witness (science) to explain how this happens. Consequently, anything else is simply speculation, for now anyway.

The last thing we need to look at in these verses is the statement, "The evening and the morning were the first day." A literal understanding of the seven days of creation, is to say the least, a little shortsighted. Since we understand the sun, stars and all of the planets are the result of an immense explosion. It would be an impossibility to cool off the earth in time for humanity to arrive literally on the sixth day.

So, to what are the seven days of creation referring? The seven days would be better thought of as, seven eons or ages of creation. So, how did we get to where we are today, if it did not happen in seven days?

"The 20th century saw a giant leap in how humans perceive the cosmos. No longer did people assume the universe was static in size. By looking at how distant galaxies recede from us, we learned the universe is expanding in volume. Tracing the expanding universe backward in time, we imagined a dense, hot beginning of our universe in a finite past. In the middle of the century, we found nuclear reactions in this hot early universe accurately account for the previously mysterious abundance of helium and deuterium. Moreover, we detected a faint afterglow of the big bang that occurred billions of years ago. The universe began with a big bang is essentially conclusive and may stand as the most profound discovery humans have ever made."[14]

Therefore, the seven days of creation are seven distinct eons, not 24-hour cycles. An eon is the largest defined unit of time. They divide into eras, which split into periods, epochs and ages. I will use the terms interchangeably in this book. Every day of creation has some distinct event, which sets it apart from the others.

> **Day 1** - Light created
> **Day 2** - Sky created
> **Day 3** - Continents & Plant Life created
> **Day 4** - Seasons created
> **Day 5** - Sea Life & Birds created
> **Day 6** - Beasts & Man created

Day 7 - God rested

The periods that I have listed are mainly geological. I say mainly because geology is a science that deals with the history of the earth and its life, especially as recorded in rocks. However, we know creation encompasses more than just the earth. Still, I believe a geological timeframe is the best match to Genesis because the Bible focuses on the formation of the earth when it speaks of creation.

Each day in Genesis may not match up perfectly with a specific geological period. However, what occurs in each day should line-up with the sequence that science has discovered.

Day 2

Genesis 1:6 And God said, Let there be a firmament in the midst of the waters, and let it divide the waters from the waters.
Genesis 1:7 And God made the firmament, and divided the waters which were under the firmament from the waters which were above the firmament: and it was so.
Genesis 1:8 And God called the firmament Heaven. And the evening and the morning were the second day.

In Day 2, we see God creating a firmament or expanse between the waters. The waters referred to here are both space and oceans. We derive that from its usage, the waters under the expanse and above it. The firmament called Heaven means the sky and clouds. Therefore, the waters above the sky would be outer space and the below it are oceans and seas.

Day 2 of the Genesis account closely coincides to the Archaean period. "It would not resemble the earth we inhabit today. The atmosphere was very different from what we breathe today; at that time, it was likely a reducing atmosphere of methane, ammonia, and other gases, which would be toxic to most life on our planet today. Also during this time, the Earth's crust cooled enough that rocks and continental plates began to form." [15]

The formation of the sky indicates that during this period the earth was starting to cool down, but not to its current state. In addition, almost everything is under water. There is no dry land. The water in this epoch was much hotter and sea life, as we know it did not and could not exist yet.

It is important to note, somewhere between the first and second day, the earth was formed. There could be no dividing of the waters, if the earth did not exist. Furthermore, if the earth exists at the beginning of the second day, then the sun has also been created.

We know from science, the sun formed before the earth. Therefore, the first day of creation included the creation of all light sources and the planets (at least earth).

I realize the moon forms on the fourth day, according to Genesis. However, our moon is not a true source of light. Moonlight is predominantly refracted sunlight. If the moon were an actual source of light, it would have no dark side.

Day 3

Genesis 1:9 And God said, Let the waters under the heaven be gathered together unto one place, and let the dry land appear: and it was so.

Genesis 1:10 And God called the dry land Earth; and the gathering together of the waters called he Seas: and God saw that it was good.

Genesis 1:11 And God said, Let the earth bring forth grass, the herb yielding seed, and the fruit tree yielding fruit after his kind, whose seed is in itself, upon the earth: and it was so.

Genesis 1:12 And the earth brought forth grass, and herb yielding seed after his kind, and the tree yielding fruit, whose seed was in itself, after his kind: and God saw that it was good.

Genesis 1:13 And the evening and the morning were the third day.

During the period of Day 3, Genesis states God created dry land. Then God said, "Let the earth produce grass, herbs and trees. What does science have to say about this sequence of events?

> "The period of Earth's history that began 2.5 billion years ago and ended 543 million years ago is known as the Proterozoic. Many of the most exciting events in the history of the Earth and of life occurred during the Proterozoic -- stable continents first appeared and began to accrete, a long process taking about a billion years. In addition, coming from this time are the first abundant fossils of living organisms, mostly bacteria and archaeans.
>
> With the beginning of the Middle Proterozoic comes the first evidence of oxygen build-up in the atmosphere. Where was this oxygen coming from? Cyanobacteria, photosynthetic organisms that produce oxygen as a byproduct, had first appeared 3.5 billion years ago, but became common and widespread in the Proterozoic. Cyanobacteria are

aquatic and photosynthetic, that is, they live in the water, and can manufacture their own food. The other great contribution of the cyanobacteria is the origin of plants.

The most striking, and important, feature of plants is their green color, the result of a pigment called chlorophyll. Plants use chlorophyll to capture light energy, which fuels the manufacture of food—sugar, starch, and other carbohydrates. Without these food sources, most life on earth would be impossible. There would still be mushrooms and algae, but there would be no fruits, vegetables, grains, or any animals (which ultimately rely on plants for their food too!)" [16]

In the beginning, science says there was dry land and plants began to form. Three days are done and the ordering of creation according to science is in absolute agreement with Genesis. So far, so good.

Day 4

Genesis 1:14 And God said, Let there be lights in the firmament of the heaven to divide the day from the night; and let them be for signs, and for seasons, and for days, and years:
Genesis 1:15 And let them be for lights in the firmament of the heaven to give light upon the earth: and it was so.
Genesis 1:16 And God made two great lights; the greater light to rule the day, and the lesser light to rule the night: he made the stars also.
Genesis 1:17 And God set them in the firmament of the heaven to give light upon the earth,

Genesis 1:18 And to rule over the day and over the night, and to divide the light from the darkness: and God saw that it was good.
Genesis 1:19 And the evening and the morning were the fourth day.

Okay we are at Day 4 and the timeline has gone a little awry. The days of creation are really eons or eras, and everything has been in sequential order, until now. The two great lights in the firmament are the Sun and the Moon. The problem is if the days of creation are sequential, then the sun came into existence in Day 1. So, why is the author reiterating the creation of light?

What we need to understand is there is a gap of time between God speaking and the physical manifestation. The first three days of creation correlate to geological eons. God is not waiting an eon before He declares the next day. This would not be very productive. Therefore, what we have is the Lord speaking in one geological stage of development and producing the next. The reality is the Bible is establishing the order of creation (starting points), not the durations. Meaning He could have spoken all seven days in quick succession and set everything in motion in the very first eon of time.

Back to our question, why reiterate the creation of light? In Day 1, God created light and separated it from darkness. The light He called day and the darkness He called night. Now, seemingly He is doing it again. So, what is going on here? During the first day, darkness already existed, before God produced anything. He only needed to create light.

The Lord initiated Life (the Big Bang) birthing stars including our Sun. Subsequently, the stars gave birth to the planets, including the earth. All of these things occurred in the eon called Day 1, approximately 8 billion years in duration. After the earth formed, daylight would come from the Sun, but the night would be almost total darkness because the Moon did not exist yet.

In Day 4, God only needed to create the Moon. Since the Sun already existed. A planet approximately the size of Mars, crashed into the earth, and created the moon, nearly 100 – 200 million years after the Sun was formed. After the moon collided with earth there was period of near total darkness, which lasted roughly 100 – 1000 years. The darkness was due to debris, vaporized rock and gas.

Following the formation of the moon, there was no light on the earth, which is why God spoke of the light by day and night. When the debris finally cleared, there was both sunlight and moon light, in accordance with God's Word.

It is interesting to note God separated light from darkness twice, the first time when He created the sun and the second time when He created the moon.

Hidden in the fourth day, is a spiritual truth. God is the one true light of the world. Anyone who abides in Him is in the light. In the beginning, humanity was with the Lord in the garden. They were continually in the light of God, but the fall of humanity plunged them into total darkness. In other words, humanity was lost.

You cannot go from absolute darkness to perfect light. The result would be blindness. The human eye needs time to adjust to either extreme. Therefore, God created the moon to light the earth. The moon symbolizes His chosen people.

Isaiah 60:2 ***For, behold, the darkness shall cover the earth, and gross darkness the people: but the***

LORD shall arise upon thee, and his glory shall be seen upon thee.
*Isaiah 60:3 **And the Gentiles shall come to thy light**, and kings to the brightness of thy rising.*

Specifically, in the Bible, this would be Jerusalem (Israel) or New Jerusalem (the Church). The moon is the only natural satellite of the earth. Meaning it revolves around the earth, to give it light. It has no light of its own. It reflects the light of the sun (primarily) and stars towards the earth. God created Israel and the Church to be a reflection of Him. They encircle the world manifesting the light of God. The purpose of these entities (Israel and the Church) is to bring the world out of darkness, gradually until the people can walk in the perfect light of God.

"It is extraordinary that the presence and nature of the Moon was essential for the development of advanced life on the Earth. The proposed theory of the moon's formation involves a collision of the young Earth with a body the mass of Mars or greater. In view of the facts that the tilt angle of the Earth's spin axis (23.5 degrees) is favorable to life, and that the mass of the large Moon is important in stabilizing that spin axis, this proposal for the Moon's formation is remarkable indeed. To produce such a massive moon, the impacting body had to be the right size, it had to impact the right point on Earth, and the impact had to have occurred at just the right time in the Earth's growth process." [17]

Science has formulated the moon was formed through a violent beginning. A quick look at the births of Israel and the Church will show they too had violent conceptions. Talk about things that make you go hmmm.

In the garden humans did not need Israel, the Church or religion. In the beginning, they only required God, our sun.

After the fall, humanity needed a way out of the darkness. Consequently, God created Israel to reflect His light. The ordering of the days in Genesis foreshadows the fall of the human race and the need for a supplemental light source.

This is also, why the scriptures construct a day as the evening and the morning. Normally, we would think the day starts in the morning and ends in the evening. However, due to sin we start in darkness and end in the light. Ending the day or age in light is a significant spiritual point of the Bible, as a whole.

In Genesis, the reason for the creation of light is for humanity to measure time (seasons, years and days) and predict weather (signs). This would have been all but impossible without the moon. The moon determined early calendars, crops and even the timing of killing animals for food.

However, the spiritual purpose though concealed in scripture, is due to the sin of humanity. God had to redo what He did in the beginning. Therefore, He formed Israel and the Church to convey signs, seasons, days and years to the world. The moon rules by night, this means we pronounce the word of God. Israel shows the light of God (the Law) and the Church displays the light of Christ (the Gospel).

Day 5

Genesis 1:20 And God said, Let the waters bring forth abundantly the moving creature that hath life, and fowl that may fly above the earth in the open firmament of heaven.
Genesis 1:21 And God created great whales, and every living creature that moveth, which the waters brought forth abundantly, after their kind, and every winged fowl after his kind: and God saw that it was good.

Genesis 1:22 And God blessed them, saying, Be fruitful, and multiply, and fill the waters in the seas, and let fowl multiply in the earth.
Genesis 1:23 And the evening and the morning were the fifth day.

A quick look at Day 5 will tell you two things emerged in this period, sea life and birds. On the other hand, science tells us that life did not go from creatures that swim to ones that fly. There are of course intermediate life forms Genesis does not mention. The writer is giving us the timespan of Day 5. Sea life marks the beginning of the period and birds indicate the end. This age in the Bible best correlates to the Paleozoic era and stretches to the Mesozoic.

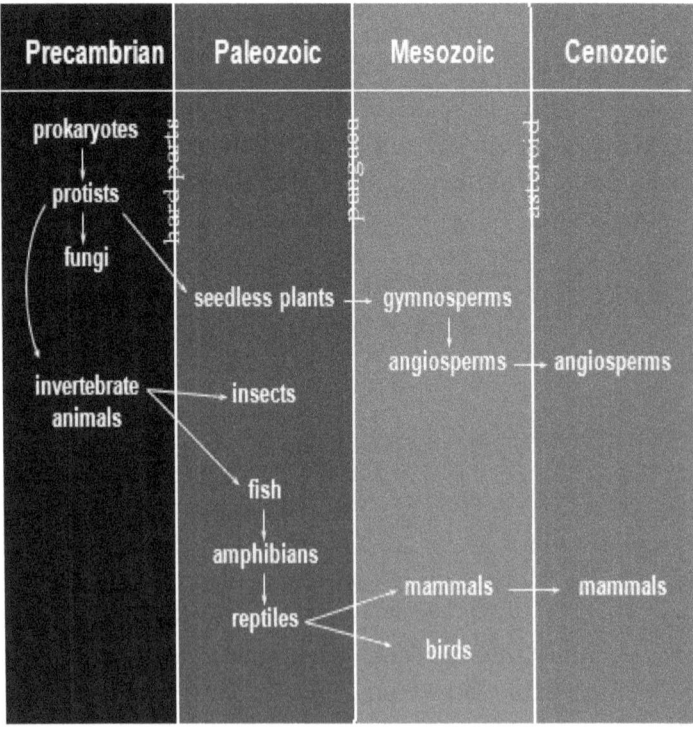

Figure 2. History of Life. Precambrian: Organisms. Retrieved on 2 August 2012, from http://faculty.clintoncc.suny.edu/faculty/michael.gregory/files/bio%20102/Bio%20102%20lectures/History%20of%20Life/history.htm

The Precambrian age in the chart is a super eon and includes the Hadean, Archaean and Proterozoic eons. It accounts for 88% of geologic time and includes Day 1 – 4 of creation. As I said, Genesis does not list everything created in Day 5. The Genesis narrative is an overview of the origins of life, not a detailed explanation.

So on the fifth day God created fish, some of which adapted into amphibians, from amphibians some changed into reptiles, then from reptiles some morphed into birds. In a nutshell, the process would be called evolution. I know that sounds like blasphemy and I risk alienating many people with this, but hear me out.

> **Evolution** - a process of continuous change from a lower, simpler, or worse to a higher, more complex, or better state.

Evolution is not anti-creation, but rather the process of creating that God chose. If the Lord had to create each domain, kingdom, phylum, class, order, family, genus and species individually, that would surely be an immeasurable waste of energy. The creator is all knowing and all wise. Therefore, it makes sense for Him to use the most effective and efficient method possible when He created life.

Think about this, as humans we create things all the time. Does evolution come into play with our inventions? Of course it does. Look at planes, cars, computers all of these things have evolved from their original form and are still evolving. Life as we know it is continuous change.

Nothing is static, not even death. Immediately after death the process of decomposition starts. In fact, crude oil comes from the remains of plants and animals, which died long ago. This indicates nothing in life remains unchanged, but everything evolves or devolves.

Since Day 5 starts with the creation of sea life and culminates with birds, this means we are looking at the evolution of vertebrate life. In other words, the period covers everything in between fish and birds, which would include dinosaurs. I know the veracity of dinosaurs is a sore subject for some, but science has concluded birds derived from reptiles, specifically the clade of Dinosauria. Before you stop-up your ears and start throwing stones, indulge me for a moment.

Every Christian worth their salt knows dinosaurs are a money making hoax. Why go into all of this evolution gobbledygook? Since we are now looking at the Phanerozoic age (Greek for "Visible Life"), it is important to know how the things we see came into existence. Figure 3 is a cladogram showing vertebrate evolution. A clade is a group consisting of a species (extinct or present) and all its descendants.

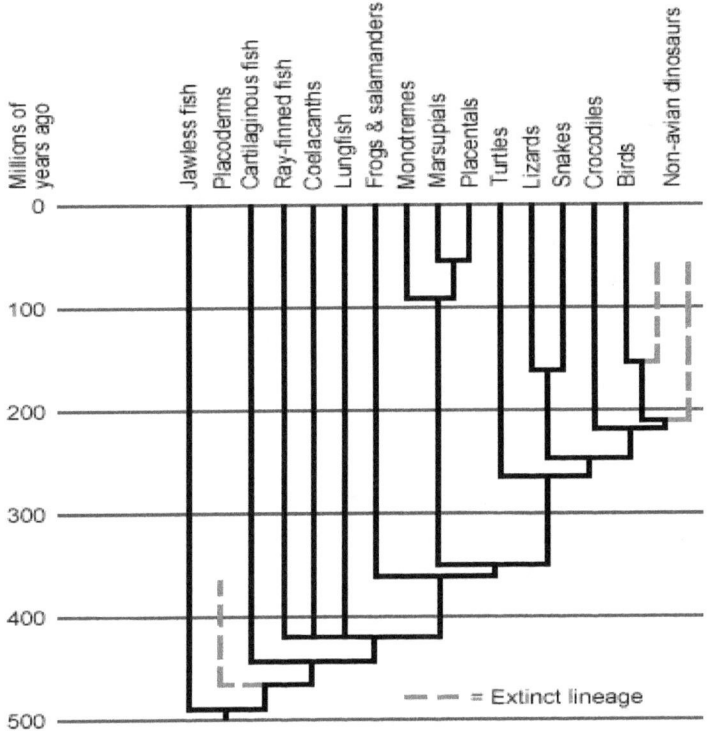

Figure 3. University of California Museum of Paleontology's Understanding Evolution. Retrieved on 3 August 2012, from http://evolution.berkeley.edu

A quick look at the chart shows turtles, lizards, snakes, crocodiles, birds and dinosaurs stem from the same lineage. I do not know about you, but turtles, lizards and crocodiles remind me an awful lot of dinosaurs.

If you go back to Figure 2, it shows birds evolving in the Mesozoic Era. Another name for this period is the Age of Reptiles. Science subdivided this era into three major periods: the Triassic, Jurassic, and Cretaceous. This is the time when dinosaurs dominated the earth. It is hard to eliminate the existence of these creatures. If we did, based on the clade we would also have to reject the reality of birds.

Okay nobody is denying the existence of birds, but dinosaurs, come on. In Genesis 1:21, it says God created great whales. This word in Hebrew is "Tanniyn", which is interpreted dragon, serpent, whale and sea monster, respectively. I think the term "Great Dragon", would be the best rendering. The Bible often uses dualistic references, one physical and the other spiritual. There are twenty-one references to dragons in the King James Version of the Bible.

On the physical side, this reference could be to dinosaurs that lived in the sea, such as the Plesiosaur (near-to lizard), Basilosaurus (king lizard) or Ichthyosaurs (fish lizard). If this is the case, then God did mention dinosaurs in the Bible. This would end the whole evolution debate, dead in its tracks. Unfortunately, no one is sure what the Great Dragon or serpent represented.

On the spiritual side, this is a direct reference to the gods of mythology. "Sea serpents feature prominently in the mythology of the Ancient Near East, attested as early as the 3rd millennium BCE (Before Common Era) in Sumerian iconography depicting the myth of the god Ninurta overcoming the seven-headed serpent. Examples of the storm god vs. sea serpent trope in the Ancient Near East can be seen with Baal vs. Yam (Canaanite), Marduk vs. Tiamat (Babylonian), and Atum vs. Nehebkau (Egyptian) among others." [18]

In these myths, there is usually a god or goddess of the sea, wreaking havoc and causing chaos in the water. When God says, He created the *Great Dragon* this nullifies the power of that deity. He is claiming supreme power over all things as creator. So, if the dragon symbolizes the god/goddess of the sea. God created it and subsequently, He has the power to destroy it. By symbolic imagery, the writer is saying the Lord is the supreme God.

In just one Hebrew word, the Lord has hidden the possible creation of dinosaurs and reduced the power of ancient myths.

Day 6 – the Creation of Beasts

Genesis 1:24 And God said, Let the earth bring forth the living creature after his kind, cattle, and creeping thing, and beast of the earth after his kind: and it was so.
Genesis 1:25 And God made the beast of the earth after his kind, and cattle after their kind, and every thing that creepeth upon the earth after his kind: and God saw that it was good.

Science calls this the Age of Mammals. We live in this current age, today. There is no day of rest (Day 7) from a geological perspective. Genesis breaks up mammals into two distinct groups, humans and everything else. If humans are mammals just like the beast of the earth, why should we segregate their origin?

We yearn to understand why we are so vastly different from every other created being. As a group and individually we reason and rationalize everything. As far as we know, Homo sapiens are the only species that seeks out its purpose in life. Unfortunately, science cannot answer this question. This is the function of religion and the aim of the Bible. Consequently, the Bible delineates the creation of mammals into two groups.

Something on a catastrophic level happened between the fifth and sixth day of creation. Large groups of marine organisms and Dinosauria went extinct. Whatever happened, it affected both land and sea. The dinosaurs disappeared around 65 million years ago, with many other land dwelling organisms also dying out around this time.

"Not all Animals died when the dinosaurs became extinct. In fact, some land mammals survived and some flourished. Why did certain animals survive, while others became extinct? The answer may lie in the feeding habits of the two groups. Most of the extinct land vertebrates were animals that lived in food chains that relied directly on living plant matter. One leading hypotheses states, the impact of an asteroid caused extinction. A dust cloud formed which blocked sunlight and killed living plants.

Other animals, including many of the mammals that lived alongside the dinosaurs, were in a different food chain. During the age of dinosaurs, most mammals were very small, shrew-like insectivores. These animals ate insect larvae, worms and small arthropods, which, in turn, feed on dead and decaying plant matter. The temporary loss of sunlight had little effect on this food chain that was dependent on dead rather than living plant matter."[19] This however is a hypothesis not a theory. This means no one has proven this yet.

"Only after the dinosaurs were gone did the mammals begin their great diversification and become the dominant land animals. Then, within 10 million years, there were mammals of all kinds living in many different habitats on land, in the sea and in the air. There were herbivores, carnivores, whales, bats. Some of them were very large, and some weighing more than about 100 pounds. During the Cenozoic there was also tremendous development in other groups including birds, reptiles, amphibians and fish, leading gradually up to the peak of biological diversity that occurred in the recent past."[20]

This fulfills the first part of Day 6. In the next section, we will attempt understand why the Bible separates humans from the other mammals (beasts).

Day 6 – the Creation of Man

Genesis 1:26 And God said, Let us make man in our image, after our likeness: and let them have dominion over the fish of the sea, and over the fowl of the air, and over the cattle, and over all the earth, and over every creeping thing that creepeth upon the earth.
Genesis 1:27 So God created man in his own image, in the image of God created he him; male and female created he them.
Genesis 1:28 And God blessed them, and God said unto them, Be fruitful, and multiply, and replenish the earth, and subdue it: and have dominion over the fish of the sea, and over the fowl of the air, and over every living thing that moveth upon the earth.

Finally, we come to the creation of humans. I think the whole concept of evolution would be acceptable to Christians if it did not include humanity. It just does not seem to mesh with making man in the image of God. On the other hand, imagine a solitary man and woman in a world full of animals of every sort, without weapons, tools or the ability to create fire. It is highly doubtful our species would have survived, outnumbered and out gunned, so to speak.

The aim of this book is not to advocate or disprove evolution. It is to substantiate the Bible's claims of creation. Therefore, we must rely heavily on the testimony of our expert witness (Science).

"God is love. Love influences the world in a persuasive rather than a coercive way and this is why chance and evolution occur. It allows the beloved, in this case the entire created cosmos, to be or to become itself."[21] This is the case with humans and all of life. God knew we would eventually sin, but He never stopped us. The freedom the Lord gives us is not unique to humanity.

All of life requires autonomy. Every living thing undergoes metabolism, possess a capacity to grow, responds to stimuli, reproduces and adapts to their environment in successive generations. Otherwise, an entity is not alive from a biological perspective. "Consequently, there must be room for indeterminacy in creation and the randomness of evolution merely highlights this fact."[22]

"If God were a magician or a dictator, then we might expect the universe to be finished all at once and to remain eternally unchanged. God did not build the world along the lines of our narrow human sense of perfection. If He did, imagine what a pallid and impoverished world that would be."[23]

In light of these facts, we must assume that humans have evolved to their present form, just like every other organism. Look at it this way, the Bible is telling us what happened and why, science gives us the how.

Genesis 1:26-28 answers two of our most vital questions. Why we are so different from every other creature and what is our purpose in life? The answer to the first question is God made us in His image, the Godhead to be specific. This is true of no other creature on earth. As to our purpose, the Bible states we are to be fruitful, multiply, replenish and subdue the earth.

The author of Genesis states God said, "Let us make man in our image, after our likeness." It is beyond the scope of science to prove or disprove this statement. Since science cannot prove or define God. It cannot verify or negate we are his representation. So, what evidence do we have regarding this declaration?

"In science because of the eternal possibility of new evidence contradicting old, a theory can only be proven false, never true. Some theories are very likely, but none of them will ever be 100% true, at least not in science.

Mathematical proof stands as an exception to this rule. Mathematics and the other sciences have a great deal in common, for example, all have the property of falsifiability. A distinction between mathematics and the other sciences is in math you can construct a true or false statement, while in other sciences you can only construct statements that are either probably true or definitely false."[24]

First, we should first define God. The scripture rather curiously says, "Let us," not "I will." Is this a translation error? No, it is not. The Hebrew word for God in this verse is "Elohim," which is the plural form of "Eloah." The syntax for God in the Old Testament takes the plural form 2249 times, but the singular only 56 times. Most of the non-plural references are in the book of Job. Why are there so many references to the plural form, when God is one? Asking this question is like opening a can of worms.

There is no agreement as to why the plural form is used. In my opinion, it seems hard to escape the fact that if God is one, then it must refer to unity and not singularity of existence. It is beyond the scope of this book to defend or dispute the doctrine of the Trinity. However, the issue is germane to the matter of man's creation. Therefore, we must choose a position. In this work, we will go with a triune view of God, for reasons that will shortly become apparent.

Mathematics uses deductive reasoning; once a theorem is proven from axioms, it is considered an absolute and permanent truth. In order to utilize math we must convert the Godhead to its numeric equivalent.

> *1 John 5:7 For **there are three** that bear record in heaven, **the Father, the Word, and the Holy Ghost**: and these three are one.*

The book of John agrees with my earlier supposition, God is one in unity, not singularity. The normal delineation of the Trinity is God the Father equals one, the Son is two and the Holy Spirit represents three.

Since we are reducing all of our terms to their numerical equivalents, what is the number of humanity? God created humans on the sixth day. Therefore, our number is six.

> *Revelation 13:18 This calls for wisdom. If anyone has insight, let him calculate the number of the beast, for **it is man's number. His number is 666.** (NIV)*

The book of Revelation confirms the number of humanity is six, by referencing the infamous 666. All of our terms have a numeric equivalent. We can now apply simple math skills to prove or disprove the statement, "Let us make man in our image, after our likeness." For this statement to be true, the Trinity of God must be equal to humankind.

Claim:	God (plural) created humans in their image and likeness.
Theory:	Father + Son + Holy Spirit = Man
Proof 1:	$1 + 2 + 3 = 6$
Proof 2:	$1 * 2 * 3 = 6$

Mathematics attests to the fact that God has created humans in his image and likeness. Biblically speaking arithmetic symbolizes temporary conditions and multiplication indicates permanency. Numerically we see God made humans in the image of the Godhead, both now and forever. However, is this just coincidence or did we tailor the numbers to fit the claim?

We cannot change what the writer of Genesis has claimed, but we can alter our assumption of what he means by the term *Elohim* (God). If the plural form of God does not intend the Trinity, then we should try to validate the statement without it. God is still equivalent to the number one and humanity remains six.

Since, one is not equal to six. What can we add to God the father? Adding anything other than God would negate the assertion of that we are created in His image.

If we hold to the theory, the Father and the Son are God, but not the Holy Spirit. This gives us the numbers one and two. If we add or multiple them, they fall short of man's number six. If we say God and His Spirit are the only real deities, but Jesus is not God. We now have the numbers one and three. Again, the math proves this conjecture is false.

I have heard a theory that *Elohim* includes God's angels. This would conflict with the scriptures assertion that humans are in God's image. Nothing else in the Bible backs up this theory. Angels are our fellow brethren in the scriptures. In addition, we do not have a numeric equivalent for angels. Consequently, there is no way to prove this biblically or mathematically.

The only view confirmed by mathematics is the Trinity. However, this does not mean all of the tenets of the Trinitarian view are correct. It simply confirms there are three distinct components to God, called *Elohim*.

It is important to note when the writer uses the term man, which in Hebrew is *adam*. It is the same as saying humankind. The term includes both male and female. This fact is critical to our understanding of Adam and Eve. We will look at it in more depth later in the book.

Before we move on we should look quickly at the purpose of humans, in verse 28. The Bible states we are to be fruitful, multiply, replenish and subdue the earth. What does this mean?

We are to be productive (fruitful) in what we do in life. This implies God intended for people to work. He also intended for us to reproduce (multiply). This speaks to not only having children, but also strategically positioning ourselves throughout the earth. Next, God tells us to replenish or refill the earth. This command is vital to understanding our identity. God initiated everything and filled the earth. He told us to refill it. The Lord predestined humans to be the gods of this world.

Consequently, there is a colossal difference between humans and other mammals (beasts).

> *St. John 10:34* ***Jesus answered them, Is it not written in your law, I said, Ye are gods?***
> *St. John 10:35 If he called them gods, unto whom the word of God came,* ***and the scripture cannot be broken;***

Jesus is quoting Psalms 82:6 where it says, "Ye are gods and all of you are children of the Most High." This is indeed a noble calling. Just because the world is ours, does not mean we should treat it anyway we want. God has entrusted the earth to us, as His children. This implies that we are to be responsible with it. The world is God's gift to us. This is what makes the Gospel good news.

We are supposed to replenish the earth's resources, not deplete them. However, it goes further than that, as the gods of this world, we are supposed to restore everything the planet is lacking. For instance, when the world seems cold and indifferent, we renew it with love. When violence is on the upswing, we re-establish peace and so on. As I said before being the god of this world implies responsibility.

The last piece of our purpose is to subdue the earth. This is a military term. It means to conquer, vanquish, defeat or overcome. "Every bird, fish and creature is to be in subjection to the authority of mankind. A conquering nature resides inside man, in order for him to subdue the earth. This is the reason that man seeks to climb the highest mountain, explore outer reaches of space and pushes himself to the limit."[25] We are also supposed to conquer or overcome our sinful nature, also known as the flesh. If you read the Letters to the seven churches in the book of Revelation, you will notice the phrase, "to him that overcomes," stated repeatedly. The most important thing to subdue in this life is our flesh (self).

Day 6 – the Diet of Man and Beast

Genesis 1:29 And God said, Behold, I have given you every herb bearing seed, which is upon the face of all the earth, and every tree, in the which is the fruit of a tree yielding seed; to you it shall be for meat.
Genesis 1:30 And to every beast of the earth, and to every fowl of the air, and to every thing that creepeth upon the earth, wherein there is life, I have given every green herb for meat: and it was so.
Genesis 1:31 And God saw every thing that he had made, and, behold, it was very good. And the evening and the morning were the sixth day.

It seems odd that the writer would include the diets of creation. After all animals eat according to instinct, only humans eat according to their whimsy. When God created humans, dinosaurs had already died off. Nevertheless, they most certainly had carnivorous breeds. As we saw earlier, mammals at first were very small and ate insects. They gradually got bigger and some became herbivores and others carnivores.

So, why mention the diets when clearly animals were never pure herbivores. God always has a reason. We will see why in the next chapters.

I heard someone state that God said, "It was good" after every creation, except humans. This of course, is not true. In fact, God said, "It was very good" at the end of the sixth day. This is the only day with that distinction and the remark is due to the creation of humans. In the first part of Day 6, after the Lord made the beasts of the earth He said, "It was good" (Genesis 1:25). Therefore, the expression refers solely to humanity.

Day 7

Genesis 2:1 Thus the heavens and the earth were finished, and all the host of them.
Genesis 2:2 And on the seventh day God ended his work which he had made; and he rested on the seventh day from all his work which he had made.
Genesis 2:3 And God blessed the seventh day, and sanctified it: because that in it he had rested from all his work which God created and made.
Genesis 2:4 These are the generations of the heavens and of the earth when they were created, in the day that the LORD God made the earth and the heavens

Finally, we come to Day 7, the end of creation. We have also crossed over into chapter two of Genesis. Chapters and verses were not originally in the Bible, publishers added them much later. Unfortunately, the end of a chapter does not always match the completion of a thought. This is the case with the first two chapters of creation. Logically, the first three or four verses belong with chapter one.

On the seventh day, God rested from His work. The whole concept of the Sabbath derives from this fact. Moses gave this commandment to the children of Israel. They were to imitate God in this respect, six days they would work, but on the seventh, rest was mandatory. Since we know the days of creation are not literal days, where are we today?

We are still living in Day 6 spiritually and have not fully entered into God's rest. Although Day 7 for God is an established fact, for humanity it is a time still in the future.

> *Hebrews 4:4* ***For he spake in a certain place of the seventh day on this wise, And God did rest the seventh day from all his works.***
> *Hebrews 4:5 And in this place again, If they shall enter into my rest.*
> *Hebrews 4:6 Seeing therefore it remaineth that some must enter therein, and they to whom it was first preached entered not in because of unbelief:*
> *Hebrews 4:7 Again, he limiteth a certain day, saying in David, To day, after so long a time; as it is said, To day if ye will hear his voice, harden not your hearts.*
> *Hebrews 4:8* ***For if Jesus had given them rest, then would he not afterward have spoken of another day.***
> *Hebrews 4:9* ***There remaineth therefore a rest to the people of God.***

The apostle Paul declares there is still a rest for the people of God to enter, where we will rest from all of our works. Therefore, Day 7 is a promised and future period for us. It can only happen after the labors of this life are finished.

Notice in verse four it does not say these are the days, but the generations of the heavens and earth. A generation implies a long time span, not a 24-hour period. This agrees with our assertion that the term day is not literal. The seven days of creation are seven distinct ages, as we stated earlier. These periods all have some distinct event that sets it apart from the others. A day in the creation narrative is closer to an eon of actual time.

The Story of Creation
(Alternate Version)

IN THE WORLD COURT
CASE NUMBER 1:01-CV-12345

THE PEOPLE, Plaintiffs
vs.
THE BIBLE, Defendant

TRANSCRIPT OF CIVIL TRIAL PROCEEDINGS OF
BENCH TRIAL
BEFORE THE HONORABLE (your name here)
WORLD COURT JUDGE

Day 1

THE COURT: Good morning to all of you. Is the Plaintiff prepared to open?

PLAINTIFF's LAWYER: Yes, I am.

THE COURT: You may do so.

PLAINTIFF: Good morning, Your Honor. I represent the plaintiffs who are challenging the Bible's claims that the world was created in seven literal days. We intend to prove "Intelligent Design" or "Creationism" has no grounds for legitimacy and should be disregarded by all rational persons. Scientific proof points to evolution as the only credible means for life as we know it today.

"An important point to remember is evolution theory, like all scientific theories, was originally a solution to a problem (Linnaean Taxonomy). What's remarkable about anti-evolution propaganda is that it never acknowledges this fact, and so never takes on the burden of producing a better explanation for that original problem.

Creationists often try to argue that God could have chosen to make the animal kingdom look that way, but they cannot explain why or how. Consequently, if they cannot explain why or how, then they actually do not have an explanation. Can anyone explain how you would derive the prediction of a "family tree" animal kingdom from the idea of God? It's not enough to say that God reused previous designs; that would explain the similarities but not the divisions in the family tree. The Linnaean taxonomy is a family tree, not a family sponge. Only evolution offers a real explanation: the kind of explanation where you can start from its mechanism and use it to logically work forward to predict the outcome."[26]

For these reasons at the end of the trial, we will request that the Court enter a finding that the Genesis account of creation is false. Thank you, Your Honor.

THE COURT: All right. Thank you. Is the Defendant prepared to open?

DEFENDANT's LAWYER: Yes, I am.

THE COURT: You may do so.

DEFENDANT's LAWYER: Good morning, Your Honor. I represent the defendant. I am confident that at the conclusion of these proceedings, you will find that the evidence shows the Bible, specifically the Book of Genesis is correct in its statements concerning creation.

The Bible is first foremost a spiritual book. Its intent is to define the purpose and relationship between God and humanity. In doing so, it defines our relationship to all of creation, including other humans. It was not written to explain the origins of the universe from a scientific perspective, but it does give a brief overview from the spiritual vantage point.

One of the main features of the Bible is its declaration that it is the Word of Truth. That being the case, time should reveal the validity of the claims in scripture. Science and Religion have been at odds for centuries, but in my opinion that should not be the case. If the Bible is stating fundamental Truths, then science should be able to corroborate at least some of its claims.

For these reasons at the end of the trial, we will request that the Court enter a finding that the Genesis account of creation is true. Thank you, Your Honor.

THE COURT: All right. Thank you. Let's begin with the first witness for the plaintiff.

PLAINTIFFS' LAWYER: Thank you your Honor. Before we call our first witness, we want to examine Exhibit 1.

Exhibit 1
Genesis 1:1 In the beginning God created the heaven and the earth.

Genesis 1:2 And the earth was without form, and void; and darkness was upon the face of the deep. And the Spirit of God moved upon the face of the waters.

PLAINTIFF'S LAWYER: Plaintiffs call Physics.

Q. What is a Physicist?
A. A physicist is a scientist who does research in physics. Physicists study a wide range of physical phenomena in many branches of physics spanning all length scales: from sub-atomic particles of which all ordinary matter is made (particle physics) to the behavior of the material Universe as a whole.

Q. Is there anything wrong with the Bible stating that God created the heaven and earth?
A. "It is reasonable to ask who or what created the universe, but if the answer is God, then the question has merely been deflected to that of who created God. In this view it is accepted that some entity exists that needs no creator and that entity is called God. This is known as the first cause argument for the existence of God."[27]

Q. Are you referring to the "Cosmological Argument"?
A. Yes.

Q. What is that exactly?
A. The *Cosmological Argument* is an argument for the existence of a "First Cause" to the universe and is often used as an argument for God. In short, it states:

1. Whatever begins to exist requires a cause.
2. The universe began to exist.
3. Therefore, the universe requires a cause.

Q. Do you dispute the "First Cause" premise?
A. Yes. Even if all three premises are true, the "First Cause" is not necessarily God. I believe the universe was created out of nothing.

Q. How could something come from nothing?
A. "Because there is a law like gravity, the universe can and will create itself from nothing. Spontaneous creation is the reason there is something rather than nothing, why the universe exists, why we exist. It is not necessary to invoke God to light the blue touch paper and set the universe going."[28]

Q. "It has been said that science provides us with a narrative as to how existence may happen, but theology addresses the meaning of the narrative. How do you respond to that?"[29]
A. "The scientific account is complete, theology is unnecessary."[30]

Q. By Theology, do you mean God?
A. Yes. "Science explains the universe without the need for a Creator."[31]

PLAINTIFF'S LAWYER: Your Honor at this time we would like to present Exhibit 2.

THE COURT: You may do so.

<u>Exhibit 2</u>

Genesis 1:3 And God said, Let there be light: and there was light.
Genesis 1:4 And God saw the light, that it was good: and God divided the light from the darkness.

Genesis 1:5   And God called the light Day, and the darkness he called Night. And the evening and the morning were the first day.

Q. In your professional opinion, could what is described in Exhibit 2 have happened approximately 6,000 years ago?
A. No, the Universe as we know it emerged from the Big Bang approximately 13.7 billion years ago.

Q. Is there any proof to support your stance?
A. "Radiometric dating the process of determining the age of rocks from the decay of their radioactive elements has been in widespread use for over half a century. There are over forty such techniques, each using a different radioactive element or a different way of measuring them. It has become increasingly clear that these radiometric dating techniques agree with each other and as a whole, present a coherent picture in which the Earth was created a very long time ago. Further evidence comes from the complete agreement between radiometric dates and other dating methods such as counting tree rings or glacier ice core layers."[32]

Q. Is the first visible piece of creation light?
A. Yes. "The Big Bang Model is a broadly accepted theory for the origin and evolution of our universe. It postulates 12 to 14 billion years ago, the portion of the universe we can see today was only a few millimeters across. It has since expanded from this hot dense state into the vast and much cooler cosmos we currently inhabit."[33] There was matter and there was antimatter. When they met, they annihilated each other and created light. Somehow, it seems that there was a tiny fraction more matter than antimatter, so when nature took its course, the universe was left with some matter, no antimatter, and a tremendous amount of light."[34]

Q. Was that light the sun?
A. No. The sun was formed around 5 million years ago or 8 million years after the Big Bang.

Q. Was there any light that was formed within the last 10,000 years? Which is the literal timeframe described in Genesis, within the approximate timeframe of biblical genealogies.
A. No, there was not. The sun, moon and the stars in our galaxy were all formed long before that timeframe.

PLAINTIFF'S LAWYER: No further questions.

THE COURT: Do you wish to cross exam the witness?

DEFENDANT's LAWYER: Yes, your Honor.

Q. You stated earlier that God was not necessary for creation to take place. Can science prove that God does not exist?
A. Science cannot prove or disprove the existence of God.

Q. I believe the real problem science has with God being the creator of the universe is the fact that it cannot define God. So, the Genesis's claim that God created the heavens and earth may be valid, but it is frustrating from a scientific standpoint. Can science prove that God didn't create the universe?
A. Since, God cannot be defined, science cannot categorically say God did not aid in its creation.

Q. Science states that the universe was created spontaneously out of nothing. Is that a true statement?
A. Yes, that is what Quantum Theory states.

Q. In Genesis 1:2, at start of creation there was only darkness. Connected to this declaration is a curious occurrence, the Spirit of God was hovering over the waters. The waters referred to here are not oceans or seas, but space. In ancient times and even today, space is likened to water. I know it is cloaked in poetic form, but we see God's Spirit hovering over darkness or nothingness just before He creates light. Couldn't this just be a pictorial means of saying God created something out of nothing?
A. It very well could be. I cannot say for sure. I am not a theologian.

DEFENDANT's LAWYER: That's okay neither am I, but I believe we all need a working knowledge of the scriptures before we can disavow them. Paul states in Hebrews 11:3 the visible things [our universe], were made from the invisible. He goes on to declare that the invisible, is God. So, according to the Bible the invisible created the visible, which science calls spontaneous creation. The ancients would have never understood Quantum Theory, for that fact, I don't think may people today understand it. I believe in this instance we could call it, "A rose by any other name." Since we know what truly matters is what something is, not what it is called.

Q. You stated earlier that the first visible piece of creation was light. So would you say that the Biblical account and science are in agreement on this point?
A. Yes, it would seem so.

DEFENDANT's LAWYER: No further questions, your Honor.

THE COURT: You may step down.

Day 2

THE COURT: Good morning to all of you. Is the Plaintiff ready to proceed?

PLAINTIFF's LAWYER: Yes, I am.

THE COURT: You may do so.

PLAINTIFF'S LAWYER: We would like to call the Court's attention to Exhibit 3.

Exhibit 3

Genesis 1:6 And God said, Let there be a firmament in the midst of the waters, and let it divide the waters from the waters.
Genesis 1:7 And God made the firmament, and divided the waters which were under the firmament from the waters which were above the firmament: and it was so.
Genesis 1:8 And God called the firmament Heaven. And the evening and the morning were the second day.

PLAINTIFF'S LAWYER: Plaintiffs call Cosmology.

Q. What is Cosmology?
A. Cosmology is the scientific study of the large scale properties of the universe as a whole. It endeavors to use the scientific method to understand the origin, evolution and ultimate fate of the entire Universe.

PLAINTIFF'S LAWYER: This issue of waters above the heavens is not only in the description of creation, but it is found in the book of Psalms. Psalms 148:4 states, "Praise him, ye heavens of heavens, and ye waters that *be* above the heavens."

Q. By definition, the firmament seems to be the sky, space or an atmospheric expanse. Is there any evidence of water above the sky?
A. No, there is not. We have not found an indication of water on the moon or Mars.

PLAINTIFF'S LAWYER: There doesn't seem to be much going on in Day 2 besides the unsubstantiated separating of waters. No further questions, your Honor.

THE COURT: Do you wish to cross exam the witness?

DEFENDANT's LAWYER: Yes, your Honor.

THE COURT: You may do so.

Q. It has been stated in this court that the definition of the word firmament is sky, space or an atmospheric expanse. Do you agree with that definition?
A. I have no reason to disagree with it.

DEFENDANT's LAWYER: During the time that the book of Genesis was written there was no such word as space. Therefore, if the Bible refers to space it must use a different term. I assert that when the scriptures refer to waters above the firmament, it is denoting what we now call outer space.

In modern times we travel to the moon in what we call a spaceship. A ship is a large seagoing vessel. We have ships in the seas, airships and spaceships. The commonality of all of these crafts is buoyancy. We can float in space as well as the water. So, Genesis is actually saying God separated outer space [waters] from the seas [waters] by the atmosphere. It has been stated in this court that the separating of waters is unsubstantiated and if I understand the plaintiff correctly, they seem to be implying that it isn't necessary.

Q. When the earth was first formed was there a need to create an atmosphere?
A. Yes. "In the beginning hydrogen and helium, the two lightest elements (gases) were by far the most abundant in the Universe. Unfortunately, earthly temperatures at start-up were very high and these gases had molecular velocities so great (greater than the escape velocity of planet Earth) that they "boiled" off into space in the early history of Earth."[35]

"After loss of the hydrogen, helium and other hydrogen-containing gases from early Earth due to the Sun's radiation, primitive Earth was devoid of an atmosphere. The first atmosphere was formed by outgassing of gases trapped in the interior of the early Earth, which still goes on today in volcanoes."[36]

Q. So, do you agree that a created atmosphere is an unsubstantiated declaration?
A. No, I do not. "Oxygen was nearly absent in the atmosphere of early Earth so photosynthesis would have created a net gain of oxygen first in the ocean and later in the atmosphere. Eventually with sufficient oxygen in the atmosphere respiration would have balanced photosynthesis except when burial removed the organic material from the oxygenated water or air. Before oxygen could build up in the atmosphere it must have oxidized reduced ions in seawater. Geologists have proven this hypothesis by examining iron deposits and the presence of detrital (formed from the products of erosion of pre-existing rocks) pyrite in sedimentary deposits older than two billion years old."[37]

DEFENDANT's LAWYER: No further questions, your Honor.

THE COURT: You may step down.

Day3

THE COURT: Good morning to all of you. Is the Plaintiff ready to proceed?

PLAINTIFF's LAWYER: Yes, I am.

THE COURT: You may do so.

PLAINTIFF'S LAWYER: We would like to call the Court's attention to Exhibit 4.

Exhibit 4

Genesis 1:9 And God said, Let the waters under the heaven be gathered together unto one place, and let the dry land appear: and it was so.
Genesis 1:10 And God called the dry land Earth; and the gathering together of the waters called he Seas: and God saw that it was good.
Genesis 1:11 And God said, Let the earth bring forth grass, the herb yielding seed, and the fruit tree yielding fruit after his kind, whose seed is in itself, upon the earth: and it was so.
Genesis 1:12 And the earth brought forth grass, and herb yielding seed after his kind, and the tree yielding fruit, whose seed was in itself, after his kind: and God saw that it was good.

Genesis 1:13   And the evening and the morning were the third day.

PLAINTIFF'S LAWYER: Plaintiffs call Geology.

Q. What is Geology?
A. Geology is the science comprising the study of solid Earth, the rocks of which it is composed, and the processes by which they evolve. Geology can also refer generally to the study of the solid features of any celestial body.

Q. Is there any plausibility to the claim land masses were formed on the third day of creation?
A. No that is much too early. "Now we need to know that fusion eventually creates heavier elements such as carbon and iron. These elements were to compose a significant part of young Earth. The pressure and heat from radioactive decay of elements and the aftershocks of massive collisions caused the Earth to be molten. Over time the surface of the Earth cooled and became the Crust."[38]

Q. In the Bible's story of creation, water always seems to have existed. Is that the case?
A. "Most of us teach earth science using simple or sophisticated models and imagery that demonstrate to students that the Earth is essentially a blue marble whose surface is dominated by oceans. This vision of a blue Earth has even been espoused by popular science writers such as the non-fiction work 'Pale Blue Dot' by the late Carl Sagan. For many it would be difficult to envision an Earth without its blue blanket of oceans. However this is precisely what the early stages of our planet were like. An ocean-free Earth existed, perhaps for several hundred million years as a consequence of extremely high surface temperatures following planetary accretion. The formation of oceans on

Earth represents no less than a global-scale cooling of Earth's surface to temperatures at which water is stable as a liquid phase."[39]

PLAINTIFF'S LAWYER: Not only did God separate the waters from the dry land, but He named the dry land "Earth" and the water He called "Seas". How could anyone substantiate a claim like that? It is impossible and that is exactly my point. The creation story is full of unsubstantiated claims. However, we want you to judge only the facts in this case. No further questions.

THE COURT: Do you wish to cross exam the witness?

DEFENDANT's LAWYER: Yes, your Honor.

THE COURT: You may do so.

DEFENDANT's LAWYER: The Bible says that God separated the waters from the dry land on the third day. We are not contending that anything in Genesis chapter one happen in a literal 24-hour period. For now let's say a day constitutes an undefined period of time. What is important here is Genesis' claim, God separated land from water.

Q. Was there a period when all water was in one place and all dry land in another?
A. "As the continents have moved through time, they have repeatedly collided to form "supercontinents." Most of the rocks that make up continents are insulators -- they are reluctant to transfer thermal energy. Eventually, heat builds up beneath the continent. The continental crust swells, stretches, and finally ruptures. New ocean floor begins to build within the rupture zones. Fragments of the supercontinent spread as the ocean plate grows along a new seafloor spreading center.

Because the Earth is a sphere, the moving continental fragments inevitably reassemble about every 500 million years."[40] So, I would have to yes there was such a period in time.

DEFENDANT's LAWYER: As far as God naming the dry land and the waters the writer is simply employing "Anthropomorphism". Throughout the Bible God is given human characteristics in order to better understand Him. We should not however, actually think God acts or reacts as we do, but we should use these types to better understand the principles given in scriptures. By God naming the waters and land, He is emphasizing His role as creator. Normally, if you create something you also name it. I believe that is the point Genesis is trying to make. No further questions, your Honor.

THE COURT: You may step down.

Day 4

THE COURT: Good morning to all of you. Is the Plaintiff ready to proceed?

PLAINTIFF's LAWYER: Yes, I am.

THE COURT: You may do so.

PLAINTIFF'S LAWYER: We would like to call the Court's attention to Exhibit 5.

<u>Exhibit 5</u>
Genesis 1:14 And God said, Let there be lights in the firmament of the heaven to divide the day from the night;

and let them be for signs, and for seasons, and for days, and years:
Genesis 1:15 And let them be for lights in the firmament of the heaven to give light upon the earth: and it was so.
Genesis 1:16 And God made two great lights; the greater light to rule the day, and the lesser light to rule the night: he made the stars also.
Genesis 1:17 And God set them in the firmament of the heaven to give light upon the earth,
Genesis 1:18 And to rule over the day and over the night, and to divide the light from the darkness: and God saw that it was good.
Genesis 1:19 And the evening and the morning were the fourth day.

PLAINTIFF'S LAWYER: Plaintiffs call Astronomy. In this exhibit, we have the Sun and Moon being created. The earth was previously somewhere in days 1 to 3.

Q. Does science concur with the Earth being formed first and then the Sun and Moon?
A. Absolutely not. All planets in our solar system are byproducts from the formation of stars.

Q. Can you explain how planets are formed?
A. "The Nebula hypothesis. Describes the probable sequence of steps in the formation of the solar system. (a) Gravitational contraction of a rotating gas cloud leads to a dense central region (eventually forming the Sun) and a more diffuse, flattened nebula. (b) Dust particles from the nebula settle onto a disc. (c) Accretion of dust into numerous small planetesimals, each a few kilometers in diameter. Collisions between planetesimals lead to capture, disintegration, or deflection of their orbits. (d) Eventually larger bodies capture the smaller ones. Uncondensed gas is

blown away by the "solar wind"; this process may begin in earlier stages."[41]

"Planets such as our own could not have formed from gas alone, but need matter in the solid phase, such as dust grains. To This process is known as accretion. The dust grains continue to accrete slowly, eventually forming clumpy "protoplanets" or "planetesimals" of a few kilometers in dimension, like asteroids. Collisions between the planetesimals eventually lead to a few larger bodies that capture smaller ones. This process is chaotic, with collisions sometimes leading to break-up of the planetesimals, changes in orbits, and often forming craters on the larger bodies."[42]

Q. Can you give us the correct sequence of formation between the earth, moon and sun?
A. The Sun was formed first and then the earth and lastly our moon formed.

Q. In your opinion, is there any possible way the earth could have been formed before the sun?
A. No it's not plausible.

PLAINTIFF'S LAWYER: No further questions.

THE COURT: Your witness.

DEFENDANT's LAWYER: Thank you, your Honor. We don't argue the fact the sun was created before the earth. The sun is the most important object to Earth. Without the sun, life could not exist. If we look closely at exhibit 5 the writer of Genesis is explaining the distinction between night and day, seasons and signs, days and years as we know them today. Nowhere does it explicitly say the sun was created on day four.

Q. You stated earlier that first the sun was created, then the earth and lastly the moon. Is this correct?
A. Yes.

Q. Do we need the moon to have night and day?
A. No, the rotation of the earth causes night and day.

Q. Do we have different seasons because sometimes the Earth is farther from the Sun and at other times, it is closer?
A. The fact that we have seasons (Spring Summer Fall Winter) on Earth is entirely due to the tilt of our North-South axis (by 23.5 degrees) relative to the orbit of the Earth around the Sun.[43]

Q. Does the moon come into play with the tilting of the axis?
A. In 1993, French mathematicians Jacques Laskar and Philippe Robutel showed that Earth's large moon has a stabilizing effect on our planet's climate. Without the moon, gravitational perturbations from other planets, notably nearby Venus and massive Jupiter, would greatly disturb Earth's axial tilt, with vast consequences for the planet's climate. The steadily orbiting moon's gravitational tug counteracts these disturbances, and Earth's axial tilt never veers too far from the current value of 23.5°.[44]

Q. So we did not experience seasons as we do today without the formation of the moon?
A. Correct.

DEFENDANT's LAWYER: Genesis 1:14 states, "Let there be lights in the firmament of the heaven to divide the day from the night; and let them be for signs, and for seasons, and for days, and years." This statement does not mean the Sun was created on day four. We might assume that if the Bible did not say light was created on day one.

Therefore, the only light we would expect to be created on day four is moonlight. The creation of the moon was through a violent collision with the earth, which caused the earth to be enveloped in an opaque rock-gas atmosphere so dense that no sunlight could reach the planet's surface for approximately 100 – 1000 years.

Since the moon has no light in itself, when the debris from the creation of the moon cleared, not only was sunlight now visible, but moonlight became visible at the same time. Science is only confirming today, what the Bible stated centuries ago. There is no conflict in the order of creation of the sun, earth and moon. No further questions, your Honor.

THE COURT: You may step down.

Day5

THE COURT: Good morning to all of you. Is the Plaintiff ready to proceed?

PLAINTIFF's LAWYER: Yes, I am.

THE COURT: Please do so.

PLAINTIFF'S LAWYER: Plaintiffs call Geology. We would like to call the Court's attention to Exhibit 6.

Exhibit 6

Genesis 1:20 And God said, Let the waters bring forth abundantly the moving creature that hath life, and fowl that may fly above the earth in the open firmament of heaven.
Genesis 1:21 And God created great whales, and every living creature that moveth, which the waters brought forth abundantly, after their kind, and every winged fowl after his kind: and God saw that it was good.

Genesis 1:22 And God blessed them, saying, Be fruitful, and multiply, and fill the waters in the seas, and let fowl multiply in the earth.
Genesis 1:23 And the evening and the morning were the fifth day.

PLAINTIFF'S LAWYER: Exhibit 6 shows whales and birds created together; there is no scientific proof to support this assertion. There is no mention of life on land and evolution contends birds developed from reptiles, not fish. I would like to present this geological chart to the court.

Era	Description	Years Before Present
Cenozoic (age of mammals)	placental mammals dominant	present — 65,500,000
Mesozoic (age of reptiles)	archaic mammals and birds replace dinosaurs	145,500,000
	dinosaurs dominant; primitive mammals spread	199,600,000
	first dinosaurs and first mammals	251,000,000
Paleozoic (ancient life forms)	spread of reptiles and insects	299,000,000
	amphibians dominant; forests flourish; reptiles and modern insects appear	359,200,000
	fish dominant; amphibians appear; first forests	416,000,000
	first land plants; fish with jaws; air breathing animals	443,700,000
	invertebrates dominant; first vertebrates (fish)	448,300,000
	invertebrates (worms, jellyfish, trilobites, etc.)	542,000,000

Figure 4. Palomar College Behavioral Sciences Department by Dr. Dennis O'Neil Retrieved on 22 February 2013, from
http://anthro.palomar.edu/earlyprimates/early_1.htm

PLAINTIFF'S LAWYER: This chart shows the generally accepted time scale of complex life forms on earth. The numbers on the right are in millions of years.

Q. Is this chart a fair depiction of the evolution process, as we understand it today?
A. Yes, the timelines are approximate, but I believe this is the general consensus.

Q. Is it possible that fish and birds appeared simultaneously?
A. Not according to fossil records collected so far, there is no evidence to support such a theory.

Q. Approximately, how far apart in years are fish from birds?
A. They are separated by as much as 302,800,000 million years.

Q. In order to bridge the gap, what would have to be included?
A. Insects, amphibians, reptiles, mammals and dinosaurs.

Q. Dinosaurs are a work of fiction to creationist from many religious backgrounds. Did they really exist in your professional opinion?
A. Yes, I base my opinion on years of scientific research and discovery.

Q. What does the term dinosaur mean?
A. The word comes from the Greek *deinos* meaning fearfully great or awe-inspiring and *sauros* means lizard or reptile.

PLAINTIFF'S LAWYER: Genesis mentions a mammal as large as the whale, but omits the awe inspiring dinosaurs.

If we are to accept that God created fish and birds, then we must include dinosaurs, according to evolution it is a package deal. No further questions, your Honor.

THE COURT: Do you wish to cross exam the witness?

DEFENDANT's LAWYER: Yes, your Honor.

THE COURT: You may do so at this time.

DEFENDANT's LAWYER: Thank you, your Honor. As I alluded to earlier, the days of creation would be better thought of as seven eons or ages of creation. A quick look at Day 5 will tell you two things were created in this period, sea life and birds. But, science tells us that life did not go from creatures that swim to ones that fly. There are of course immediate life forms that are not mentioned. Genesis is not going to describe every distinct life form. So, why did the Bible skip over something as big as dinosaurs?

I believe the writer is giving us a scale of creation in Day 5. Sea life marks the beginning of the period and birds indicate the end. This day in the Bible best correlates to the Paleozoic era and stretches to the Mesozoic, as indicated in the plaintiff's chart.

Q. If day 5 represents what I just mentioned; does it go against evolution and your understanding of how life formed?
A. No it does not.

DEFENDANT's LAWYER: Since I believe the writer of Genesis is giving us a span of creation in day 5, there is no need to mention dinosaurs per se. In addition, the term dinosaur was first introduced in 1842 by the English biologist and paleontologist Sir Richard Owen, long after the book of Genesis was written. However, the word interpreted whale in Hebrew is "Tanniyn", which is means dragon, serpent, whale and sea monster, respectively. The overwhelming translation is dragon, which occurs 21 times in the King James Version of the Bible. This begs the question, what is a dragon? A dragon is a mythological representation of a reptile. The common depiction of them in art, shows they resemble a giant lizard.

Q. You already testified the word dinosaur means great lizard, is that correct?
A. Yes, that is correct.

DEFENDANT's LAWYER: Therefore, the great dragon spoken of here may very well be a description of dinosaurs. This means Genesis does include these creatures in its span of creation. No further questions, your Honor.

THE COURT: You may step down.

Day6

THE COURT: Good morning to all of you. Is the Plaintiff ready to proceed?

PLAINTIFF's LAWYER: Yes, I am.

THE COURT: You may do so.

PLAINTIFF'S LAWYER: We would like to call the Court's attention to Exhibit 7, which is our last. We have purposely skipped verses 29 and 30 of Genesis, since they deal with diet and not creation. Also, we are not including the seventh day as evidence, since creation stops at day six.

THE COURT: Is that okay with you?

DEFENDANT's LAWYER: Yes, your Honor that is fine.

THE COURT: You may proceed with you exhibit.

<u>Exhibit 7</u>

Genesis 1:24 And God said, Let the earth bring forth the living creature after his kind, cattle, and creeping thing, and beast of the earth after his kind: and it was so.

Genesis 1:25 And God made the beast of the earth after his kind, and cattle after their kind, and every thing that creepeth upon the earth after his kind: and God saw that it was good.

Genesis 1:26 And God said, Let us make man in our image, after our likeness: and let them have dominion over the fish of the sea, and over the fowl of the air, and over the cattle, and over all the earth, and over every creeping thing that creepeth upon the earth.

Genesis 1:27 So God created man in his own image, in the image of God created he him; male and female created he them.

Genesis 1:28 And God blessed them, and God said unto them, Be fruitful, and multiply, and replenish the earth, and subdue it: and have dominion over the fish of the sea, and over the fowl of the air, and over every living thing that moveth upon the earth.

Genesis 1:31 And God saw every thing that he had made, and, behold, it was very good. And the evening and the morning were the sixth day.

PLAINTIFF'S LAWYER: Man evolved just like every other animal, insect and mammal we have seen so far. This took millions of years to happen, not the 6000 or so years from the proverbial Adam and Eve to the present day. Man was formed through evolution not shaped from the earth and breathed on by God as religion tells us.

DEFENDANT's LAWYER: Objection. Nowhere in exhibit 7 does it talk about Adam or forming man from the earth, which is in another chapter of Genesis.

THE COURT: Sustained.

PLAINTIFF'S LAWYER: I retract my last statement. We call Paleoanthropology to the stand.

Q. What is Paleoanthropology?
A. Paleoanthropology is the study of human origins.

Q. In Genesis 1:26 it says, "Let us make man in our image, after our likeness." Is it possible that man was excluded from evolution and formed differently?
A. No. "Early man was consisted of a morphologically diverse group of hominids. The majority of anatomical, archaeological and genetic evidence give credence to the view that fully modern humans are a relatively recent evolutionary phenomenon."[45]

Q. Is it feasible to believe that we started with two people approximately 6000 years ago and have come to our current population?
A. No. "It has been claimed the current world population could be produced from only two people in 6,000 years, using the appropriate exponential arithmetic. The fallacy in this claim, of course, is that the human population has not

been growing at a steady rate. This is a classic One-Sided Equation, failing to consider factors that limit the population. Human population is limited mainly by its ability to feed itself, and until the past few hundred years, that limitation (combined with humanity's lower ability in the past to cope with natural catastrophes) has kept the population steady and fairly low. Only recently have we had the technology to remove these environmental limitations, resulting in a population explosion. Therefore, it is not valid to extrapolate the current rate of growth, which is much less affected by its past limitations, back in time."[46]

Q. Did humans evolve from monkeys?
A. No. "Humans and great apes had a common ancestor about 5 million years ago. Humans and monkeys had a common ancestor about 50 million years ago. Nowhere, except in the most illiterate anti-evolution literature, will you find a claim that humans evolved from monkeys."[47]

Q. Evolution is just a theory. Does that mean scientists are guessing at the origins of man?
A. People often use "theory" to mean a guess or unsubstantiated idea about how something works. An idea that hasn't been confirmed is called a hypothesis, which is a guess. A theory is a hypothesis that is testable and backed by evidence, which has been repeatedly confirmed through observation and experiment. So, evolution is not a guess, but a solid scientific statement.

Q. So, let me be absolutely clear, mankind evolved into its present state, we did not originally look like we do today?
A. That is correct, we evolved to our present state.

PLAINTIFF'S LAWYER: Thank you. No further questions, your Honor.

THE COURT: Your witness (motioning to the defendant).

DEFENDANT's LAWYER: Thank you, your Honor. The mechanisms of evolution like natural selection and genetic drift work with the random variation generated by mutation. The plaintiff is claiming man is a product of evolution and therefore not created specifically by God, but he is a random occurrence.

Q. Is the following number sequence random: 5926535897932384626433383279?
A. Yes, it appears so.

DEFENDANT's LAWYER: You are correct. "It not only looks random, but it is random. Does it also imply it is meaningless? No. These are the digits of pi beginning with the fourth decimal place. Random does not equal "meaningless." The scientific meaning of random is that something cannot be predicted with better accuracy than that predicted by statistics. The phenomenon is its own simplest description. Biological systems are far too complex to describe or predict mathematically. We have incomplete information, and significant events like climate change or asteroid impact that are unpredictable."[48]

Albert Einstein stated, "God does not play dice with the universe." Genesis 1 gives us the specific purpose or meaning for humanity, not our detailed origins.

Q. Can evolution tell us the purpose of man?
A. No.

Q. Does the theory of evolution eliminate God?

A. No. "There is no evidence to show that God was not the guiding force behind evolution. Common descent could describe the process used by God. Until the discovery of a test to separate chance and God this interpretation is a valid one within evolution."[49]

Q. Does evolution mean God did not create the universe and everything in it?
A. No. "Evolution cannot say exactly why common descent chose the paths that it did."[50]

DEFENDANT's LAWYER: No further questions, your Honor.

THE COURT: You may step down. The court will now hear the plaintiff's closing arguments.

PLAINTIFF'S LAWYER: Thank you, your Honor. "When Charles Darwin introduced the theory of evolution through natural selection years ago, the scientists of the day argued over it fiercely, but the massing evidence from paleontology, genetics, zoology, molecular biology and other fields gradually established evolution's truth beyond reasonable doubt. Today that battle has been won everywhere, except in the public imagination. Embarrassingly, in the 21st century, in the most scientifically advanced era the world has ever known, creationists can still persuade politicians, judges and ordinary citizens that evolution is a flawed, poorly supported fantasy. They lobby for creationist ideas such as "intelligent design" to be taught as alternatives to evolution in science classrooms."[51]

Creationism is at best a hypothesis, but it fails to be testable or provable. Conversely, the theory of evolution has been proven by its testability. Therefore, I am requesting that the jury enter a finding that the Genesis account of creation is false, due to lack of proof.

THE COURT: The court will now hear the defendant's closing arguments.

DEFENDANT's LAWYER: Thank you, your Honor. "How are we to understand the Genesis story of creation in six days? We need to remember that The Bible has no interest in how God made the world. It is interested in why he made it. The six days etc., of the Genesis story are the symbolical context for various great truths, which have made the account meaningful even to the uneducated over the centuries.

The Bible is not, and does not pretend to be, a scientific textbook. It is a history of salvation. As we have seen there is no conflict between established scientific theories and biblical truth."[52] In fact, science is the proof that validates Genesis. At no point have we during this proceeding shown the scriptural account to be incorrect. For a text as ancient as the Bible, I find that nothing short of amazing. Therefore, I am requesting the jury enter a finding that the Genesis account of creation is indeed true.

THE COURT: Do you have anything further before we adjourn these proceedings?

PLAINTIFF'S LAWYER: Nothing more your Honor.

DEFENDANT's LAWYER: Nothing more your Honor

THE COURT: Members of the jury, now that you have heard all the evidence, it is my duty to instruct you on the rules that applies to this case. It is your duty to weigh and to evaluate all the evidence received in the case and, in that process, to decide the facts. You must decide the case solely on the evidence and the law and must not be influenced by any personal likes or dislikes, opinions, prejudices, or sympathy. You will recall that you took an oath promising to do so at the beginning of the case.

You must follow all these instructions, not single out some, and ignore others; they are all important. Please do not read into these instructions or into anything I may have said or done any suggestion as to what verdict you should return—that is a matter entirely up to you.

THE COURT: Has the jury reached a verdict?
(Remember you are also the jury)

THE JURY: Yes, your Honor.

THE COURT: What is your verdict?

The Garden of Eden

Genesis 2:4 These are the generations of the heavens and of the earth when they were created, in the day that the LORD God made the earth and the heavens
Genesis 2:5 And every plant of the field before it was in the earth, and every herb of the field before it grew: for the LORD God had not caused it to rain upon the earth, and there was not a man to till the ground.
Genesis 2:6 But there went up a mist from the earth, and watered the whole face of the ground.
Genesis 2:7 And the LORD God formed man of the dust of the ground, and breathed into his nostrils the breath of life; and man became a living soul.

Immediately when we read in Genesis 2:4, "These are the generations of the heavens and of the earth when they were created," we understand the writer is referring to the seven days of creation previously described in chapter one. Notice it does not say these are the "days," but the "generations" of the heavens and earth. The Hebrew word for days is "Yom" used in Genesis 1:14. The Hebrew word for generation is "Dor." The word "Dor" is always associated with birth and that is the context here. This is the birth of the heavens and earth. Therefore, each day of creation is actually a generation or birth of a period in history. This interpretation agrees with the findings of science as to the origins of the universe.

Before we go on, let me define a few terms. "The word myth has been wrongly used to mean folklore and legend. A myth is a sacred story from the past, which is concerned with the powers that control the human world and the relationship between those powers and human beings. A folk tale is a story which is pure fiction and which does not have a particular time or space. It is usually a symbolic way of presenting the way human beings cope with the world where they live. A legend is a story from the past about a historical individual. These stories are concerned with people, places, and events in history."[53] That being said what we are looking at in Genesis chapters one would be a Jewish creation myth.

"The mythologies of all the world's people are designed to answer such questions as "Who are we as a people?" " How did we originate?" and "Why do we die?" Created by Jews and adopted by Christians, the Genesis creation story has had an exceptionally long and complex history, which cannot be explored in the scope of this book.

It was about a century and a half ago that scholars first noted that Genesis seemed to contain two distinct creation stories, using different names for the creator (translated here as "God" and "the Lord"), with different emphases (physical vs. moral issues), and even a different order of creation (plants before humans, plants after humans). Scholars whose religious faith does not require them to believe otherwise have since generally agreed that the grand but starkly simple poetic opening of Genesis was the product of a much later period than the story of what traditionally is called "the Fall."

The first narrative states themes typical of mature Judaism: the creator is the sole ruler of the universe, and even in the process of creation, he has provided the foundation for the Jewish Sabbath. Although it rejects the typical polytheism of Mesopotamian creation stories like the Enuma Elish, it shares certain features with them: land emerging out of an original watery chaos and waters above and beneath the earth. In Genesis, speech calls the world into being, and speech blesses it. The concept of the divine Word of God was to be a central concept of Judaism, later adopted by both Christianity and Islam."[54]

"The main differences between the two accounts, whose sources reflect different epic traditions, are the names of the deity: Genesis 1, *Elohim* (God - plural); Genesis 2, *YHWH* (Jehovah - singular); In the first account the creation of plants (Genesis 1:11 third day) precedes the creation of man (Genesis 1:26, sixth day), but in the second before man there was no shrub in the field and the grains had not yet sprouted (Genesis 2:5–7), trees being created only after the creation of man (Genesis 2:8–9); In Genesis 1:20–21, 24–25 animals were created before man, but in Genesis 2:19, after man; The creation of man is repeated in the second account, but whereas in Genesis 1:27 male and female were created together, the woman was fashioned from a rib of the man in Genesis 2:21. The second account does not mention the creation of day and night, seas, luminaries, marine life, but commences immediately with the forming of man from the dust of the earth."[55]

In order to deal with the apparent inconsistencies theologians have come with several theories. The view that is most persuasive among critical scholars of the Pentateuch (first five book of the Old Testament) is the Documentary Hypothesis, or the Graf-Wellhausen Hypothesis, after the names of the 19th-century scholars who put it in its classic form. This theory says there are four distinct narratives, Jahwist (J), Elohist (E), Priestly (P) and Deuteronomist (D).

> **The "J" source** — the Yahwist. J gets its name because it uses and allows humans to use the name (Jahwe in German) before Israel exists (see Genesis

4:26; cf. E and P, below). J appears to have been composed in Judah, perhaps during Solomon's day, around 950 B.C.E.

The "E" source — the Elohist. The name is derived from E's use of Elohim (Hebrew for "God") rather than YHWH in the early period. E reserves the name Yahweh for the time from Moses on (see Exodus 3:13-15). E appears to have been written in the north, around 850 B.C.E.

The "P" source — the Priestly source. P is especially concerned with stories and laws relevant for priests. Like E, it reserves the name YHWH for for the period from Moses on (see Exodus 6:3). Many scholars date P either during the exile (6th century B.C.E.) or shortly after (5th century B.C.E.). Others date it as early as the beginning of the 7th century B.C.E.

The "D" source is essentially the book of Deuteronomy. It is not mingled with J, E and P.

Tradition holds Moses as the author of the Pentateuch. Whether it was Moses or several other authors who originally penned the first five book of the Law, it should be of little consequence.

2 Timothy 3:16 ***All scripture is given by inspiration of God****, and is profitable for doctrine, for reproof, for correction, for instruction in righteousness:*

2 Peter 1:20 Knowing this first, that no prophecy of the scripture is of any private interpretation.
2 Peter 1:21 ***For the prophecy came not in old time by the will of man: but holy men of God spake as they were moved by the Holy Ghost.***

If we take the stance that God divinely inspires all scripture, then I believe we can correctly begin to interpret the scriptures. That being the case, I am not going to view this as two separate accounts of the creation narrative, but as one cohesive unit.

Notice, Genesis 2:5-7 is not saying there were no plants or herb on the earth until man. Verse five starts off with the word "and" which is a conjunction connecting it to verse four. If we read them together it states, these are the generations, in which God made the earth and heavens and every plant, herb before they were in the earth. This is to say God designed them in His mind, before they manifested on the earth. The author goes on to say in the beginning it did not rain. In spite of this, a mist from the ground watered the plants and during this timeframe, humans did not exist yet.

The author is describing the beginning of the water cycle. The first stage of the water cycle is evaporation/transpiration (mist). Then we have condensation (cloud formation) and after that, we get precipitation (rain and/or snow). The recap of creation ends with the appearance of humanity.

With all of the major events associated to creation, why does the summary only include plants, herbs and humanity? Here we are shifting the attention away from creation of the universe, to our next subject the Garden of Eden. The focus in this story is humanity and the plants they eat and cultivate.

Genesis 1 tells us God made man in His image and after His likeness, specifically the Godhead or Trinity. In chapter two verse seven, the writer goes further by saying humans were formed from the dust (dirt) of the ground and

God breathed into them the breathe of life. In other words, the image of God is internal, not external. The breath used to animate humans, formed the image and likeness of God inside of them. Man (male and female) did not become a living spirit, but a conscious soul. Therefore, what makes us truly alive is the combination of Spirit and flesh (dust of the ground).

We are not pure spirit wrapped in a body. If we were, then at death we would be our true selves. We would be free of the limitations of the body and would never want to go back to our original state. However, the apostle Paul says it is just the opposite.

> *2 Corinthians 5:1 For we know that if our earthly house of this tabernacle were dissolved, we have a building of God, an house not made with hands, eternal in the heavens.*
> *2 Corinthians 5:2* **For in this we groan, earnestly desiring to be clothed upon with our house which is from heaven:**
> *2 Corinthians 5:3 If so be that being clothed we shall not be found naked.*
> *2 Corinthians 5:4 For we that are in this tabernacle do groan, being burdened: not for that we would be unclothed, but clothed upon, that mortality might be swallowed up of life.*

The book of second Corinthians declares that we will passionately crave a new heavenly body, after death (even now). In Paul's first letter to the Corinthians, he compares our bodies to seeds sown into the ground. His point is the seed sown into the earth is always notably different from the plant that springs forth afterwards.

> *1 Corinthians 15:44* It is sown a natural body; it is raised a spiritual body. **There is a natural body, and there is a spiritual body.**
> *1 Corinthians 15:45* And so it is written, **The first man Adam was made a living soul; the last Adam was made a quickening spirit.**
> *1 Corinthians 15:46* Howbeit that was not first which is spiritual, but that which is natural; and afterward that which is spiritual.
> *1 Corinthians 15:47* **The first man is of the earth, earthy: the second man is the Lord from heaven.**
> *1 Corinthians 15:48* As is the earthy, such are they also that are earthy: and as is the heavenly, such are they also that are heavenly.
> *1 Corinthians 15:49* And **as we have borne the image of the earthy, we shall also bear the image of the heavenly.**

Only through Paul do we see why Genesis 2:7 is relevant to anything. Now we have our natural bodies in the semblance of Adam, but our new bodies will be in the similitude of Christ (the last Adam). The writer slipped this little nugget right under our noses.

Earlier while we were looking at how God formed man, the verse goes on to say He breathed into his nostrils. I however, used the plural while explaining the text. The Hebrew word for man is *adam*. When God created man or Adam, He created both male and female.

> *Genesis 1:26* And God said, **Let us make man** in our image, after our likeness: **and let them** have dominion over the fish of the sea, and over the fowl of the air, and over the cattle, and over all the earth, and over every creeping thing that creepeth upon the earth.

Genesis 1:27 **So God created man in his own image**, *in the image of God created he him;* **male and female created he them**.

Notice when God created man the pronoun "them" occurs, not once but twice. This is not an accident. The writer is implicitly telling us man (Adam) represents both male and female. This is an important, but overlooked fact when studying the Garden of Eden. However, there is a scripture in Genesis most never read.

Genesis 5:1 This is the book of the generations of Adam. **In the day that God created man**, *in the likeness of God made he him;*
Genesis 5:2 **Male and female created he them;** *and blessed them,* **and called their name Adam**, *in the day when they were created.*

The writer is now explicitly telling us that term Adam refers to both male and female. He sums it up by saying, God called their name Adam. This fact blows away our Sunday school understanding of Adam and Eve. I will repeatedly underscore the fact that Adam is both male and female, in effort to reinforce the truth in your psyche. Whatever the woman known as Eve represents, we know for sure she is not a literal female.

Genesis 2:8 And the LORD God planted a garden eastward in Eden; and there he put the man whom he had formed.
Genesis 2:9 And out of the ground made the LORD God to grow every tree that is pleasant to the sight, and good for food; the tree of life also in the midst of the garden, and the tree of knowledge of good and evil.

Genesis 2:10 And a river went out of Eden to water the garden; and from thence it was parted, and became into four heads.

Genesis 2:11 The name of the first is Pison: that is it which compasseth the whole land of Havilah, where there is gold;

Genesis 2:12 And the gold of that land is good: there is bdellium and the onyx stone.

Genesis 2:13 And the name of the second river is Gihon: the same is it that compasseth the whole land of Ethiopia.

Genesis 2:14 And the name of the third river is Hiddekel: that is it which goeth toward the east of Assyria. And the fourth river is Euphrates.

Genesis 2:15 And the LORD God took the man, and put him into the garden of Eden to dress it and to keep it.

Genesis 2:16 And the LORD God commanded the man, saying, Of every tree of the garden thou mayest freely eat:

Genesis 2:17 But of the tree of the knowledge of good and evil, thou shalt not eat of it: for in the day that thou eatest thereof thou shalt surely die.

The first thing we see is God doing what appears to be work. He is planting a garden in the east part of Eden. In the beginning of the chapter, He was resting from all His work of creation. So, is this another recap of Day 6 or are we looking at a different timeframe? I believe we are still looking at sixth day of creation in verse eight and this ends the dispensation. Verses nine through fourteen are descriptive passages that give us details of Eden and its garden. At this point God is finished all of his creative work and enters His rest, Day 7. Then verse fifteen picks up where we left off in verse eight, with *adam* both male and female moved to the garden. After relocating to Eden, God commands them not to eat from the tree of the knowledge of good and evil.

We need to try to decipher what is going on in this text. God created a garden and placed Adam in it. It states that a river flows through Eden and in the middle of the garden. There it branches off into four tributaries (Pison, Gihon, Hiddekel and Euphrates). No one has ever found to my knowledge the Pison or Gihon Rivers. We do however know the Euphrates and Tigris (Hiddekel) rivers are located in the Middle East. Although we do not know the location of the Gihon River, the scripture states it compasses the whole land of Ethiopia. This means that Eden covers two continents, Africa and Asia. This would also make Eden a kingdom, due to its size. We know the garden is in the east. From a biblical perspective, Jerusalem would be the best candidate for the garden, because God throughout the Bible chooses to dwell in this city. The problem is Jerusalem does not have four rivers coming out of it.

No one at any time in history has pinpointed the location of the Garden of Eden. I believe it is because we are looking at a legend. This is the legend of Adam. In chapter one, we were dealing with a creation myth, which we found to be completely accurate. Now we are dealing with a different form of writing.

"As a literary device or artistic form, an allegory is a narrative or visual representation in which a character, place, or event can be interpreted to represent a meaning with moral or political significance. Authors have used allegory throughout history in all forms of art to illustrate or convey complex ideas and concepts in ways that are comprehensible or striking to its viewers, readers, or listeners.

Writers and speakers typically use allegories to convey hidden or complex meanings through symbolic figures, actions, imagery, or events, which together create the moral, spiritual, or political meaning the author wishes to convey. Many allegories use personification of abstract concepts."[56]

If we assume the Garden of Eden is a symbolic narrative. This might explain why no one has ever found it. We still need to understand the symbols, messages and truths contained in this sacred text, in order to ascertain the spiritual meaning behind it.

First, we should look at Adam's relationship to the garden. We have God planting a garden in Eden and placing humans in it. The Hebrew word for garden is "Gan," which can mean an enclosed garden, figurative of a bride or garden of plants. I believe the garden is an enclosure, in this particular instance. Why is it not, a real garden?

"Genesis 2:15 is commonly taken to mean that God's original purpose for man in the garden was to work it and be a steward of it. This interpretation is incorrect given certain grammatical, exegetical, and theological considerations."[57]

> *Genesis 2:8 And the LORD God planted a garden eastward in Eden; and there he **put** [Hebrew word "sum"] the man whom he had formed.*
>
> *Genesis 2:15 And the LORD God took the man, and **put** [Hebrew word "Nuach"] him into the garden of Eden to dress it and to keep it.*

"The Hebrew word translated 'put' in verse eight is different from verse fifteen. In verse 8, the word translated as 'put' is the general Hebrew word "sum." However, in verse 15 it is "Nuach" meaning 'rest', which is where we derive the name Noah. The term generally has two uses, God's safety which he gives to people in the land or the dedication of something before the presence of the Lord. Further, the sense of the verb is causative, meaning that God "caused Adam to rest" in the garden."[58]

So, if Adam is in a literal garden to rest and not work, who is going to perform the upkeep? Gardens are a lot of work and if man is just there to rest, then it does not seem to be very practical. Here is where we need to start making some connections. We have two ways to start, either God is giving Adam safety or He is dedicating something to him. There are no scripture references to Adam being in safety. However, God does present him with something. Before we try to look at that, we have another dilemma before us.

"The problem is the pronoun ('it') in verse fifteen does not agree in gender with the word garden. Since pronouns have to agree with their antecedents in number and gender, the pronouns (pronominal suffixes to the verbs) here cannot be referring to the word garden. The endings of the verbs (pronominal suffixes) are feminine but the word 'garden' is masculine in Hebrew. Thus, 'garden' cannot be the object of the verbs.

There is no word in the context, which agrees in gender of the verb endings. There are only two options in understanding the grammar here. One, Genesis 2:15 indicate an exception to the rule that pronouns have to agree with their antecedents in gender. Two, the seeming inconsistency of the genders indicates that the verbs are not referring to the garden and that something else is meant by the grammar."[59]

> *Genesis 2:15 And the LORD God took the man, and put him into the **garden** of Eden to dress **it** and to keep **it**.*

Simply stated, when we translate verse fifteen from Hebrew to English the pronoun 'it' logically goes with the noun garden. The word "it" does not exist in Hebrew. We derive it from the verbs that precede it (no pun intended). The problem is Hebrew assigns gender (masculine and feminine) to words, just like Spanish. The verbs "dress" and "keep" are both feminine, in essence making "it" feminine. Now "it" cannot be associated to the word garden ("Gan" in Hebrew) because it is masculine. In fact, all of the nouns in this verse are masculine. They say ignorance is bliss. I know I was happier just knowing the English translation.

What did God give to Adam? In Genesis 2:22, the Lord presents Adam with a woman. She is his help meet. Later, man changes her name to Eve. We know Eve is Adam's wife, so logically she is the bride and the "it" of verse fifteen.

Now we have another dilemma. How can God give the Woman to Adam for a wife, when Adam represents both male and female? How does creating this woman give them rest? We definitely need to decipher who or what this woman represents.

According to the scriptures, there are two Adams. The first, God made from the earth and the second came from heaven. Now it is clear why the writer added, the Lord formed man from the dust (dirt) of the ground, in Genesis 2:7. The first Adam is in contrast to the last and there is no mistaking the two.

> *Romans 5:14* **Nevertheless death reigned from Adam** *to Moses, even over them that had not sinned*

> *after the similitude of Adam's transgression,* **who is the figure of him that was to come.**
> *Romans 5:15 But not as the offence, so also is the free gift. For if through the offence of one many be dead, much more the grace of God, and the gift by grace,* **which is by one man, Jesus Christ**, *hath abounded unto many.*

> *1 Corinthians 15:45 And so it is written,* **The first man Adam** *was made a living soul;* **the last Adam** *was made a quickening spirit.*
> *1 Corinthians 15:46 Howbeit that was not first which is spiritual, but that which is natural; and afterward that which is spiritual.*
> *1 Corinthians 15:47* **The first man is of the earth, earthy: the second man is the Lord from heaven.**

Jesus is the last Adam. He restores everything the first one lost. Therefore, we should apply our question to the last Adam. Did God present Him with a woman, to be His wife? I can already hear people saying, the Church.

> *Revelation 21:2 And I John saw* **the holy city, new Jerusalem**, *coming down from God out of heaven,* **prepared as a bride adorned for her husband.**

New Jerusalem is almost synonymous with the Church, but it is not the Church. New Jerusalem is a holy city that incorporates all of God's people. This includes those from the Old and New Testament. In other words, it is Israel and the Church.

In the book of Revelation, we have the last Adam given rest with His bride, New Jerusalem. The woman represents a city, in this case. How does this pertain to the first Adam? Could the woman God gave him also be a city? If so,

Adam could still signify both male and female. We will come back to this later in the chapter, after God creates the woman.

Now we will turn our attention to the river flowing out of Eden to water the garden and becoming four branches. Our assumption at this point is we are looking at the legend of Adam. Eden may or may not be an actual place. Since no one has found it to date, we will deem it not to be a physical region. So what do Eden and its garden represent?

We know the features. It has a river that flows into four. We also know it has two items symbolized as trees. This means they should look similar to each other. While looking through some images online I stumbled across something that stopped me in my tracks. It was diagram of the human brain and at the bottom of the image, there was the logo A.D.A.M. with some sort of plant. I immediately started searching for the meaning of this acronym to see if they knew something, I did not. A.D.A.M. stands for "Animated Dissection of Anatomy for Medicine," just a coincidence. Nevertheless, it got me thinking outside of the box, as far as the Garden of Eden goes. I cannot show the picture I saw due to copyright issues, but I have two images that will illustrate the same thing, minus the logo.

Blood is supplied to the brain by two arteries, the internal carotid artery (ICA) and the vertebral artery. The ICA supplies circulation to the anterior (front) of the brain. The vertebral arteries flow into and form the basilar artery. These two arteries supply circulation to the posterior (back) of the brain. The posterior communication artery connects the blood flow from the front and back of the brain. This connection forms what is called the Circle of Willis in the middle of the brain.

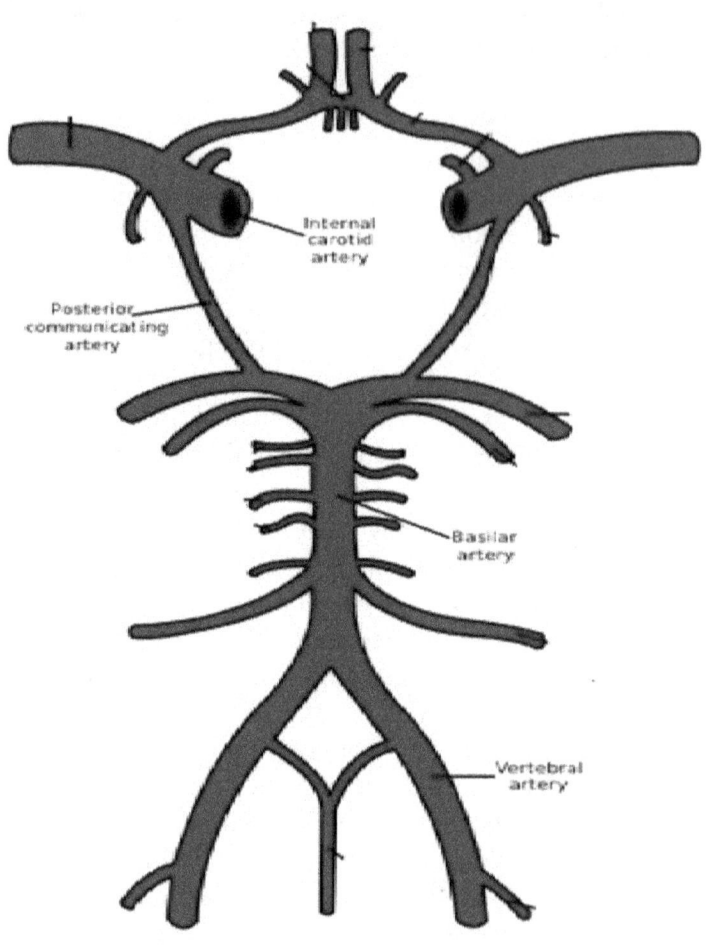

Figure 5. Artery: Basilar Artery. Wikipedia. Retrieved on 3 April 2013, from http://en.wikipedia.org/wiki/Basilar_artery

In Figure 5, the vertebral artery (river 1) on the left and right converge into the basilar artery (river 2). The internal carotid artery (river 3) on the left and right merge into the posterior communicating arteries (river 4) forming the circle of Willis, where all four rivers connect. I think the four arteries, sort of look like a stick figure of a man inside the brain. Figure six, shows their location in the brain.

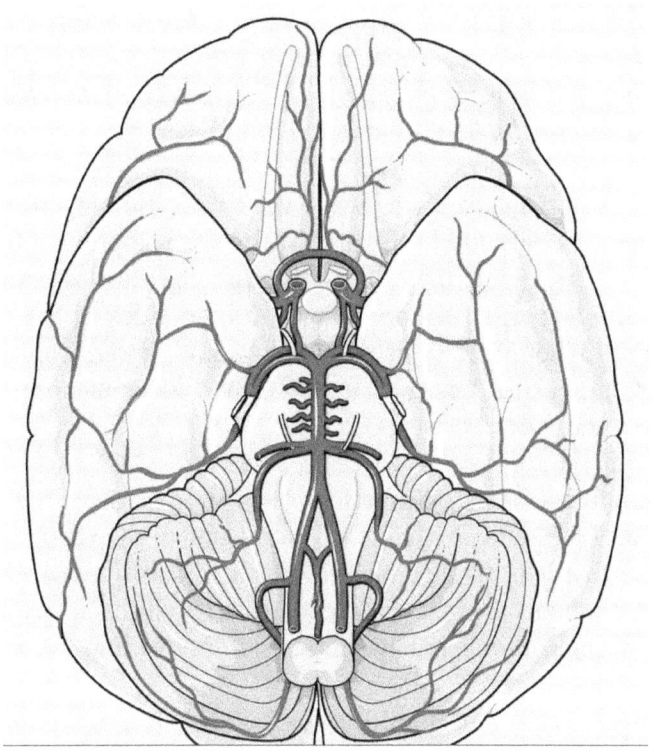

Figure 6. Drawing Arteries brain.
Anatomytool. Retrieved on 19 May 2023, from
https://anatomytool.org/content/servier-
drawing-arteries-brain-inferior-view-no-labels

The Circle of Willis is in the middle of the human brain. It may be a stretch, but stay with me for a minute. I believe the two hemispheres of the brain are the tree of Life and the Tree of Knowledge of Good and Evil. The Basilar artery is the river that branches into four heads. Remember, whatever we find should parallel Christ the last Adam.

Revelation 22:1 **And he shewed me a pure river of water of life**, *clear as crystal, proceeding out of the throne of God and of the Lamb.*
Revelation 22:2 **In the midst of the street of it, and on either side of the river, was there the tree of life,** *which bare twelve manner of fruits, and yielded her fruit every month: and the leaves of the tree were for the healing of the nations.*

In New Jerusalem, there is a river of life flowing from the throne of God. On both sides of the river, there is a tree of Life. The blood that flows through the basilar artery is literally a river of life to us and on both sides of the artery there is a hemisphere of the brain. Think about it, if this is the Garden of Eden, then it was right under our nose, so to speak and we never suspected it.

There is one more enigma to solve. If one side of the brain is the Tree of Knowledge of Good and Evil, what does it mean to eat from it? We will explore that question in the next chapter. I hope that you are still willing to read that far, because things are starting to get interesting.

Genesis 2:18 And the LORD God said, It is not good that the man should be alone; I will make him an help meet for him.
Genesis 2:19 And out of the ground the LORD God formed every beast of the field, and every fowl of the air; and brought them unto Adam to see what he would call them: and whatsoever Adam called every living creature, that was the name thereof.
Genesis 2:20 And Adam gave names to all cattle, and to the fowl of the air, and to every beast of the field; but for Adam there was not found an help meet for him.

When we look at these verses, it is imperative that we remember what we covered in Genesis chapter one, namely males and females collectively are called Adam (man). In addition, the beast of the field and every other creature, God created before man existed. Here is the kicker, everything God created evolved and that takes time. Many years have elapsed between Genesis chapter one and where we are now.

Imagine that Adam is a male, for a minute. Do we really believe God created man as an asexual being or did He realize late in the process this was not beneficial for man? This would mean woman was an afterthought of God. Are we implying the Lord is dull-witted? If the helper mentioned here is a female complement to Adam, what does that say about the all-knowing Creator? The literal explanation is problematic in reference to God.

The scripture says Adam gave names to all of the creatures, which means he could talk. How did he develop a language in isolation? "In his famous course of lectures at the University of Geneva (1906-1911), de Saussure distinguished language as a system. It is a cultural institution, spoken and heard by individuals: language is not complete in any speaker [individual]; it exists only within a collectivity...only by virtue of a sort of contract signed by members of a community."[60]

In other words, one individual alone cannot create a language. Therefore, it would be impossible for one person to name animals, if no one else existed.

I assert the creatures of the earth received their names from the male and female, called Adam. Together they named all creatures of the earth. We should take it a step further. I know this goes against conventional teaching, but if humankind has evolved to the point of speaking and we know language takes time to develop. Would it be realistic for one couple to be alone on the earth?

Logically, there must be people scattered everywhere. If this were the case, other females would have to exist prior to Eve, in order to propagate the earth. God commanded man to be fruitful and multiply in Genesis chapter one. How could he obey the Lord without a female counterpart? Just some food for thought, as we continue to unfold the narrative.

Genesis 2:21 And the LORD God caused a deep sleep to fall upon Adam, and he slept: and he took one of his ribs, and closed up the flesh instead thereof;
Genesis 2:22 And the rib, which the LORD God had taken from man, made he a woman, and brought her unto the man.
Genesis 2:23 And Adam said, This is now bone of my bones, and flesh of my flesh: she shall be called Woman, because she was taken out of Man.
Genesis 2:24 Therefore shall a man leave his father and his mother, and shall cleave unto his wife: and they shall be one flesh.
Genesis 2:25 And they were both naked, the man and his wife, and were not ashamed.

The language in this text is very figurative and we should not interpret it literally. Here we have the creation of Adam's wife. The Woman God created is not a person, but a city, as we alluded to earlier. The deep sleep Adam experienced lasted for a number of years, in order to build a city. The Hebrew word for "deep sleep" is "Tardemah." It could mean a trance like state, which would be brief, or it could be for a longer undisclosed period.

*Isaiah 29:10 For the LORD hath poured out upon you **the spirit of deep sleep, and hath closed your eyes: the prophets and your rulers, the seers hath he covered.***

In the book of Isaiah, God placed Israel and its leaders in a deep sleep. The prophet starts in verse one of Isaiah saying add year to year, meaning this has been going on for quite some time. He goes on to say Israel has been in a deep sleep and this is why they do not understand what is going on. The writer is implying if they were awake then they would comprehend. The point is the term "deep sleep" means a long period, in this instance.

So, if God is not performing the world's first surgery on Adam, what is going on? The writer is using the woman and marriage as an allegory to symbolize the Holy City of God and their relation to it. I realize this is a new concept. Religion has taught us that Adam and Eve are the first man and woman on earth. This belief is embedded in our psyche. However, if this is true, how did Cain their son know how to build a city?

*Genesis 4:17 **And Cain** knew his wife; and she conceived, and bare Enoch: and he **builded a city, and called the name of the city, after the name of his son, Enoch.***

If Cain lived in a city before God expelled him from the garden, then it would be natural for him to build another one. Accordingly, I believe the Woman depicted here is really the Holy City. This means the text is describing the first (or one of the first) civilization. Adam called the city Eve, because she was an integral part of him.

Genesis 2:23-24 cements the man wife ideology in our minds, because we use these verses in our marriages. The text, "Bone of my bone and flesh of my flesh," resonates with us when we are in love and want to get married. It is hard to wrap our minds around the fact that all of this is in reference to a city. In spite of this, look at the following scriptures.

> *Genesis 2:24* **Therefore shall a man leave his father and his mother, and shall cleave unto his wife: and they shall be one flesh.**

> *Ephesians 5:31* **For this cause shall a man leave his father and mother, and shall be joined unto his wife, and they two shall be one flesh.**
> *Ephesians 5:32* **This is a great mystery: but I speak concerning Christ and the church.**

When the Bible talks about something being a mystery, it is referring to a spiritual truth that has been hidden somewhere in the scriptures. The apostle Paul declares this passage is a great mystery. Therefore, we should endeavor to understand it.

I spoke of this in the prologue, but it bears repeating. Most people take a literal view of the Garden of Eden story. This turns the allegory into a historic narrative, which leads to all sorts of problems.

<u>Golden Rule of Interpretation</u>
When the plain sense of scripture makes common sense, seek no other sense.

There are two reasons why this rule should not be followed for Adam and Eve. The first reason is we are looking at an allegory. An allegory is a symbolic narrative in which the surface details imply a secondary meaning. The secondary meaning is the true intent of the story. The second reason we should not use the golden rule of interpretation is God routinely hides things in His Word.

Proverbs 25:2 ***It is the glory of God to conceal a thing****: but the honour of kings is to search out a matter.*

How do Adam and the Eve relate to Christ and the Church and what is God concealing in this story?

In the book of Genesis, we have the first Adam in the garden and Paul tells us that Jesus is the last Adam (1 Corinthians 15:45-47). Since Christ is the last Adam, if we look closely at how they parallel, this should give us the true (secondary) meaning of the narrative.

1. God causes Adam to sleep and opens his side
2. The Woman is formed from Adam
3. God presents the Woman to Adam as his bride

<u>God causes Adam to sleep and opens his side</u>
First, God causes Adam to fall into a deep sleep and then He opens up his side. What is the significance of this action? In the Bible, the term deep sleep is figurative of death. By opening the side of Adam, God is symbolically taking the breath or life from him to create the Woman.

Most translations state God took one of Adam's ribs and made a woman. "However, according to Ziony Zevit, Distinguished Professor of Biblical Literature and Northwest Semitic Languages at American Jewish University in Bel-Air, California, "rib" is the wrong translation for *'tsela'* in the story of Adam and Eve. He believes that it should be translated as "a non-specific, general term," in other words, simply side."[61]

In parallel, God caused Jesus to fall into a deep sleep, which indicates His death on the cross. This was also the work of God. John states, "For God so loved the world that he gave his only begotten Son." After, Jesus the last Adam is in a deep sleep, His side is also opened.

> *St. John 19:33* **But when they came to Jesus, and saw that he was dead already**, *they brake not his legs:*
> *St. John 19:34* **But one of the soldiers with a spear pierced his side**, *and forthwith came there out blood and water.*

The blood is for the remission (canceling) of our sins and the water cleanses us. These are the components of the Spirit of God. By pouring out the blood and water from Jesus, God is symbolically taking the life from Him to create the Church. The first Adam relates to the physical creation of the Woman. The last Adam correlates to the spiritual formation.

The Woman is formed from Adam

God creates the Woman from Adam. Remember, the Bible declares, ādām is a term denoting both male and female. God created the Woman, but she cannot be a literal female, since the gender already exists.

Think about this, would God command Adam to be fruitful and multiply (Genesis 1:28), without giving him the means to reproduce? That would be putting the cart before the horse, so to speak. Do we think God has dementia, of course not?

It is important to note, the Hebrew word "Asah" translated "made" is used in the creation story for every living thing God created, except the formation of the Woman.

The Hebrew word "Banah" is used for the Woman, which means to build. This is the first time we see the word used in the Bible, the next place is Genesis 4:17 when Cain builds a city. Curiously, the Woman is built, but the rest of creation is made.

> *Genesis 2:22 And the rib, which **the LORD God** had taken from man, **made [built] he a woman**, and brought her unto the man.*

To build means to form by ordering and uniting materials by gradual means into a composite whole. This means it took some time to form the Woman. It was not an instantaneous manifestation, which is why Adam needed to be in a deep sleep.

What did God build from Adam? The Woman represents a city. Since she is built from Adam prior to the original sin, the city is therefore holy. This is the original Holy City of God, long before Jerusalem. Can we prove this assumption? Yes, what is true of the first Adam must also be true of the last one.

This assumption if proved will turn our understanding of the garden event upside down. If the Woman is a city, then there were many people in the garden, when the serpent spoke.

God created the Church by opening the side of the last Adam (Jesus). This entity was also built.

*St. Matthew 16:18 And I say also unto thee, That thou art Peter, and **upon this rock I will build my Church**; and the gates of hell shall not prevail against it.*

The building of the Church is also a gradual work. The Church was not presented to Jesus immediately after His resurrection. It is still a future event. Concerning the Church the apostle Paul states, Jerusalem above is our mother (Galatians 4:22-26). This means, New Jerusalem is the city and the Church members represent the inhabitants. However, the two terms are interchangeable. Therefore, building the Church and building the city New Jerusalem are indistinguishable.

Jesus told His disciples that He was going away to prepare or build a place for them (St. John 14:2-3). The Woman He is building is New Jerusalem. There is a definite duality in Jesus' roles. As the last Adam He is still in a deep sleep, but as our Lord He is building His bride.

As I stated earlier, what is true of the first Adam must be true of the last. Therefore, since the Woman represents the Holy City with Jesus, the same must be true of the first Adam. This is indeed a *Great Mystery*, as Paul has declared.

<u>God presents the Woman to Adam as his bride</u>
In the last point, after Adam is awakened God presents the Woman to him as his bride. Adam declares the Woman is bone of his bone and flesh of his flesh, meaning the two are one.

Subsequently, Adam renames the Woman and calls her Eve, because she is the mother of all living. Paul declares the same concerning the Church. He states, Jerusalem above is the mother of all of us.[62]

In parallel to the first Adam, New Jerusalem comes down from God out of heaven, prepared as a bride for Christ (Revelation 21:2).

	First Adam	**Last Adam**
Taken from Adam's side	Bone and Flesh	Blood & Water
Woman formed from Adam	Physical	Spiritual
God presents bride to Adam	First Holy City (Eve)	Last Holy City (New Jerusalem)

In the beginning God stated, "It is not good that the man should be alone; I will make him a help meet for him." We now realize that the term translated in this scripture as man is actually the Hebrew word "ādām", which means male and female. It looks like God is saying it is not good for humans to be in isolation. In other words, we need community.

However, it is much more than that. The Woman was created to be a help meet for Adam (male and female). First, we must understand there is no such thing as a "Helpmeet", which we render as "Helpmate" today. Helpmeet is not a word. The phrase is "help meet", which are two separate words. The word meet is archaic English term, meaning suitable, right or proper. However, the footnote from the original King James Version has a notation indicating the meaning in Hebrew was "as before him". This means the term meet actually has the connotation of face to face.

Let's take a closer look at the word help. In Hebrew, the word is "Ezer". The meaning of this word is not simply help, but "succor". An *Ezer* helps in times of hardship or distress. The Hebrew word is used 21 times in the Old Testament. Almost every instance of "Ezer" is used to describe God.

When we see the Lord is our help, we understand the term to mean a very strong help. "Ezer" was not intended to evoke images of docility, subservience or even equality. Quite the opposite it carries the connotation of military might, power or an unstoppable force that is greater than the individual. If the Woman is an actual female and females are considered the weaker sex, how can she be the *Ezer*?

The help meet that God created for Adam was the Holy City (Woman). The city that was built from Adam (male and female) was meant to be a mighty power and advocate for humanity. This is why Jesus spoke of us saying, "We will do His works and even greater works." The greater works is what the body of Christ carries out. Jesus could only do so much physically because of the limitations of time and space, but the Kingdom of God is virtually unlimited.

Christ carries the thought of an "Ezer" forward with the Holy Spirit. He said He would leave us the "Comforter", which is better translated Helper. Just as God in the Old Testament was our help in the times of hardship or distress; The Holy Ghost is our ever present Help today.

A woman in the Bible can represent a great city. We are explicitly told this truth in Revelation 17:18, "the woman which thou sawest is that great city, which reigneth over the kings of the earth." Let's look at some more witness to this fact.

The Woman	Great City	Group
Genesis 2:22-23	Eve	Eden
Galatians 4:22-26	Jerusalem	Israel
Galatians 4:22-26	Jerusalem Above	All Believers
Revelation 12:1-2	Jerusalem	Israel
Revelation 17:3-4	Rome	Church
Revelation 21:2	New Jerusalem	All Believers

The mystery of the Woman is that she is the city of God and not an actual female. Therefore, males and females are equals, as far as God is concerned.

The rest we referred to in Genesis 2:15 for Adam (humans), comes from residing in the holy city. Due to the fall of humanity, this rest was never realized. Jesus did not give us this rest during His first Advent (Hebrews 4:8-9). Our rest comes when we dwell in the holy city, called New Jerusalem.

The whole purpose of Jesus' ministry is restoration. How can Christ the last Adam restore the Holy City to us, if the first Adam never had one? Think about it. If New Jerusalem is only replacing the current one, what part do we (Gentiles) have in it? Jerusalem is the Holy City of Israel, not the Church. I know God includes us by faith via Christ. However, Jerusalem holds little relevance to non-Jews. By that, I mean it is not our homeland.

In addition, we did not lose Jerusalem through Adam's sin. Jesus Christ came to restore what was lost, due to the fall of man. Every other covenant and work of God is towards this end. Therefore, I contend Adam's bride in the garden was the original Holy City of God.

The last verse in this chapter states, both man and his wife were naked and not ashamed. This of course is a poetic way to state it was a period of innocence. We would expect this type of composition in the city of God. Next, we will turn our attention to the origin of sin.

The Fall of Man

Genesis 3:1 Now the serpent was more subtil than any beast of the field which the LORD God had made. And he said unto the woman, Yea, hath God said, Ye shall not eat of every tree of the garden?
Genesis 3:2 And the woman said unto the serpent, We may eat of the fruit of the trees of the garden:
Genesis 3:3 But of the fruit of the tree which is in the midst of the garden, God hath said, Ye shall not eat of it, neither shall ye touch it, lest ye die.
Genesis 3:4 And the serpent said unto the woman, Ye shall not surely die:
Genesis 3:5 For God doth know that in the day ye eat thereof, then your eyes shall be opened, and ye shall be as gods, knowing good and evil.

Now we are ready to deal with the topic of the original sin. Since we have already turned the common understanding of Eden upside down, there is no need to stop now. If the Woman is a not a literal female, can the talking serpent be real? Who or what is the serpent?

> *Revelation 12:9 And* ***the great dragon was cast out, that old serpent, called the Devil, and Satan****, which deceiveth the whole world: he was cast out into the earth, and his angels were cast out with him.*

That was easy. Easton' s Revised Bible Dictionary states, "It has been well remarked regarding this temptation: "A real serpent was the agent of the temptation, as is plain from what is said of the natural characteristic of the serpent in the first verse of Genesis chapter three and from the curse pronounced upon the animal itself. But that Satan was the actual tempter, and that he used the serpent merely as his instrument."

If we go with the premise that the garden is physically located in the brain as I alluded to in the last chapter, then the serpent cannot be real, unless we have snakes in our heads, like the Greek goddess Medusa. Why did the writer choose a snake of all things? In ancient times, the serpent was an emblem of cunning and wisdom. Today, we would use an owl to speak to the woman and there would be no confusion.

It is time to start making some connections again and use our deductive skills. If the garden story is a legend, then so are the characters in the narrative. The only characters in this account that existed prior to its start are Adam (male and female) and God. Every other entity is representative of something else.

> The serpent is in the garden and the serpent represents the Devil.
> The garden is physically located in our brain.
> Therefore, the Devil is in our head.

This argument is only valid if both the premise and conclusion are true. For that reason, it is imperative that we test our reasoning. On the surface, the conclusion seems to say the Devil is imaginary. If nothing I have said so far has caused you to stone me, this train of thought just might do it. I hope not, just hear me out.

If the serpent does not represent a fallen angelic being, who or what does it embody? The serpent in this narrative appears to be a natural part of the story. Notice, the Woman talks freely back and forth without the slightest apprehension. At no point in history, have woman freely associated with snakes.

Since the garden is located in the brain, what familiar entity can converse naturally with us? I submit the serpent represents our rationale mind.

Let's see how well this concept fits. Man (the rationale mind) is more subtle (intelligent) than every other creature that God created. This is talking about creatures made on the sixth day. Man is by far the wisest and most cunning of the entire creation. How does intelligence tie into talking to ourselves?

Actually, interacting with ourselves is a sign of self-awareness. It shows that we seek insight into our own actions. Talking to ourselves is a critical part of humanness and evidence that we are a higher species.

In addition, look how the conversation starts, the serpent says, "Did God really say, you must not eat from any tree in the garden." (New International Version) It is as if they were already having a discussion. This would be unnatural to anyone, but the mind. Otherwise, we would expect the Woman to say, excuse me did I miss something, were we having a conversation earlier?

Furthermore, notice the Woman never reprimands or questions the serpent for challenging God. The serpent's motives never come into play. This is because everything said, is an internal dialogue. Remember the Woman is not a person, but the Holy City (people of God). Since cities are not animated, the Woman represents the inhabitants.

"Most of us talk to ourselves, silently, the majority of the time. This nearly continuous conversation is so much a part of our everyday experience that we rarely notice or remark on it. Our inner voices express our thoughts, bringing them into our awareness. It is, indeed, hard to imagine life without the inner voice. Because our inner voice formulates our thoughts, we quite naturally view it as central to consciousness and tend to assign it a special sort of authority and truthfulness."[63]

This is exactly what the Woman did, when she relied on the authority of her inner voice, over the voice of God.

Genesis 3:6 And when the woman saw that the tree was good for food, and that it was pleasant to the eyes, and a tree to be desired to make one wise, she took of the fruit thereof, and did eat, and gave also unto her husband with her; and he did eat.
Genesis 3:7 And the eyes of them both were opened, and they knew that they were naked; and they sewed fig leaves together, and made themselves aprons.
Genesis 3:8 And they heard the voice of the LORD God walking in the garden in the cool of the day: and Adam and his wife hid themselves from the presence of the LORD God amongst the trees of the garden.

Listening to our inner voice is a perfectly normal part of life. Nevertheless, when we give our voice a higher level of authority than the voice of God, it becomes sin. The Woman was clear on the commandment she received from the Lord. It was not an accident. She began to rationalize the validity of what God said, compared to what she saw.

Before we move on, we should define sin. The Hebrew term for sin is *"Hattat"* which means missing of a standard, mark, or goal. We must understand that God is the creator of everything, even standards of morality. Everything God created has a specific function and purpose. Laws or standards derive from His intent. Anything we do that goes against our purpose is sin.

Therefore, to sin is to miss the mark or goal that God has created for us. According to Genesis chapter one, humans were created in the image and likeness of God. Therefore, if God is love, then our purpose is to love. Consequently, whatever we do that obstructs love is sin to us. The commands of God are righteous because they keep us in line with our divine function and purpose.

We are now ready to look at what we call the "Original Sin." In order for there to be an original sin, there must an initial commandment. As Paul said, "Sin is not imputed when there is no law."[64] If one of the hemispheres of the brain represents the tree of Knowledge of Good and Evil, then the Woman could not have literally eaten the fruit. What command could she break, if there is no physical tree? As far as we can see, God only gave Adam two commands.

1. Genesis 1:28 And **God blessed them, and God said unto them, Be fruitful, and multiply, and replenish the earth, and subdue it: and have dominion** over the fish of the sea, and over the fowl of the air, and over every living thing that moveth upon the earth.

2. Genesis 1:29 **And God said, Behold, I have given you every herb bearing seed**, which is upon the face of all the earth, **and every tree, in the which is the fruit of a tree yielding seed; to you it shall be for meat.**

The Woman did not violate the first commandment. This is evident by fact there were enough people to constitute a city. Even today, humans have taken dominion over everything they can see, including each other, which was not part of the first commandment.

However, history tells us the humans violated the second command. How did they disobey God? Humans at some point began to eat meat. Could all of this fuss be over eating meat?

It really should not seem that farfetched, when most people believe the original sin was eating an apple. The Bible never mentions apples, so I am not sure how we ever pinpointed this particular fruit in the first place. So, what is the big deal about eating meat? After all, it is just protein, right?

"Somewhere way back in history, a threshold was crossed. In the evolutionary backwoods of the brain, something unprecedented happened in the story of life on Earth. The human brain changed and was suddenly able to compute, manage and store information like never before."[65] But, why did our brains change?

It was a new meat diet, full of densely packed nutrients, which provided the catalyst for human evolution, particularly the growth of the brain, states Katharine Milton, a physical anthropologist and authority on the primate diet.

"Craig Stanford biological anthropologist and professor of Anthropology and Biological Sciences at USC make the assertion, our large brains gave us our exceptional thinking capacity and other distinctive characteristics, including advanced communication, tool use, and walking on two legs. Or was it the other way around? Did the challenges faced by early humans push the species toward communication, tool use, and walking and, in doing so drive the evolutionary engine toward a large brain? According to Stanford, what made humans unique was meat. To be more exact, it is cooking of flesh foods.

Specifically, humans desire for meat, the eating of meat, the hunting of meat, and the sharing of meat. Perhaps because it provides a highly concentrated source of protein--essential for the development and health of the brain--meat is craved by many primates, including humans."[66]

Science seems to corroborate meat eating had a significant impact on the size and thinking ability of the human brain. The Bible puts it this way, "the eyes of them both were opened and they knew they were naked."[67] At this point in the story, they hid from God. Where did they hide? They hid among the trees, meaning they hid behind their human reasoning. In other words, they made excuses, as we will soon see.

Genesis 3:9 And the LORD God called unto Adam, and said unto him, Where art thou?
Genesis 3:10 And he said, I heard thy voice in the garden, and I was afraid, because I was naked; and I hid myself.

Here we see humans are no longer innocent, but they immediately feel shame for their actions. Children run around naked and feel no shame, even though everyone around them is wearing clothes. We teach them not to run around naked, because it is improper. Once they have this knowledge of good and bad actions cemented in their psyche, they will never freely roam unclothed again. This is what happened to us in the garden. We ate from the tree of Knowledge of Good and Evil and now our minds will always judge between the two. Unfortunately, once innocence is lost it can never been regained.

Since all of this stemmed from eating meat, does God want us to be vegetarians? No, if we believe this, then we are missing the real point. If God's eternal purpose is for us to be meat free, Jesus would have been a vegetarian from birth. Jesus said, "The Son of man came eating meat and drinking; and you say, Behold a gluttonous man, and a winebibber, a friend of publicans and sinners!"[68] Furthermore, Christ gets right to the point in the book of Mark.

> *St. Mark 7:18 And he saith unto them,* ***Are ye so without understanding*** *also?* ***Do ye not perceive, that whatsoever thing from without entereth into the man, it cannot defile him;***
> *St. Mark 7:19* ***Because it entereth not into his heart, but into the belly, and goeth out into the draught, purging all meats?***

If eating meat cannot defile us, why did God make all the fuss about eating meat in garden? God expelled Adam and Eve from paradise over meat. However, now we can eat everything under the sun without spiritual repercussions. Am I missing something?

There is one fundamental law that governs the world. It is the law of reciprocity. Every living thing on the planet adheres to the law of sowing and reaping, without exception. Reciprocity is the law, for all life on this planet and it is always in force. God put this law in place to benefit humanity. One seed produces countless pieces of fruit. This law enables humans to operate like Him, by faith. By simply planting our word through faith, we would almost effortlessly reap a bountiful harvest.

The fall of man caused us to experience the bad side of reciprocity. Prior to the fall, humans were sinless and could sow only good seeds. Once we became familiar with evil, we immediately began to reap its harvest. This set the course of humanity on fire.

Once humans started killing animals in order to eat, we inadvertently sowed the seeds of violence and murder. After the fall, the next tragedy we see is the murder of Abel by his brother Cain. It has been this like this, ever since. This is why God commanded Adam to eat as an herbivore. Adam as the god of the earth violated his purpose by killing. By doing so, he reaped a harvest he never envisioned.

How could humans disobey God? The Woman rationalized, if they ate meat they would not die. How did the people of the Holy City come to this conclusion? Either they watched animals eating their prey or they saw other people eating meat (people outside of Eden).

Remember, there were people around before Adam. The narrative states, God placed man in the garden, which means he existed somewhere else first.

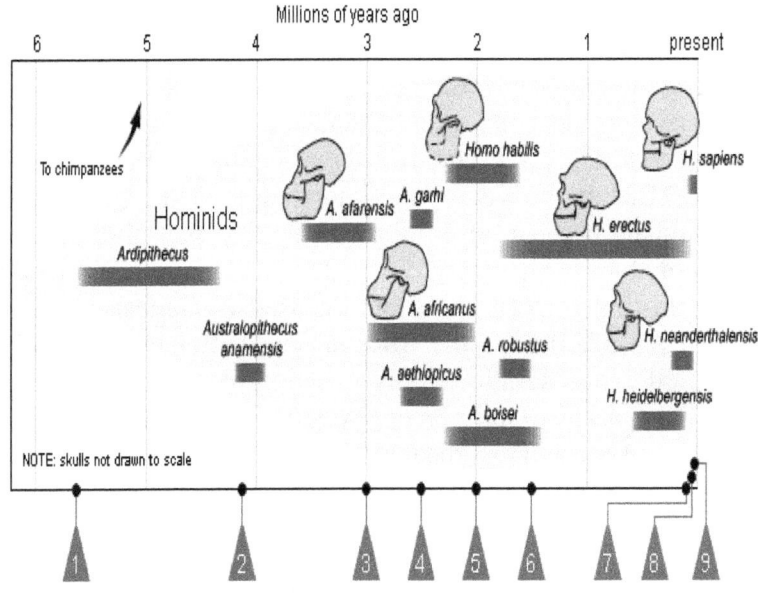

Figure 7. Human Evolution. University of California Museum of Paleontology Retrieved on 9 April 2013, from http://evolution.berkeley.edu/evosite/evo101/IIE2cHumanevop2.shtml

"The earliest documented members of the genus *Homo* are *Homo habilis,* which evolved around 2.3 million years ago; the earliest species for which there is positive evidence of use of stone tools. The brains of these early hominids were about the same size as that of a chimpanzee.

During the next million years a process of encephalization (increased brain mass) began, and with the arrival of *Homo erectus* in the fossil record, cranial capacity had doubled to 850 cm. *Homo erectus* and *Homo ergaster* were the first of the hominids to leave Africa, and these species spread through Africa, Asia, and Europe between 1.3 to 1.8 million years ago. It is believed that these species were the first to use fire and complex tools."[69]

The inhabitants of Eden could have seen either *Homo erectus* or *Homo ergaster* eating meat and concluded that they would not die as a result. The fallacy is in the interpretation of the commandment. God said in Genesis 2:17, "But of the tree of the knowledge of good and evil, thou shalt not eat of it: for in the day that thou eatest thereof thou shalt surely die." The Hebrew word for day used in this verse is the same on used in Genesis chapter one. We determined the word day in that chapter actually referred to a generation or dispensation of time, not a literal 24 hour period. God's Word was true as we saw with the murder Abel. This means, the conclusion the Woman reached was erroneous.

Genesis 3:11 And he said, Who told thee that thou wast naked? Hast thou eaten of the tree, whereof I commanded thee that thou shouldest not eat?
Genesis 3:12 And the man said, The woman whom thou gavest to be with me, she gave me of the tree, and I did eat.

Genesis 3:13 And the LORD God said unto the woman, What is this that thou hast done? And the woman said, The serpent beguiled me, and I did eat.
Genesis 3:14 And the LORD God said unto the serpent, Because thou hast done this, thou art cursed above all cattle, and above every beast of the field; upon thy belly shalt thou go, and dust shalt thou eat all the days of thy life:
Genesis 3:15 And I will put enmity between thee and the woman, and between thy seed and her seed; it shall bruise thy head, and thou shalt bruise his heel.

Adam (male and female) and the Woman answered God from among the trees. As I said before this means they were rationalizing their responses to the Lord. Immediately we have the blame game. God asked the man, who told you that you were naked? He wanted to know where they acquired the knowledge. They admitted the Woman gave it to them. Next, He asked the Woman, what have you done? She responded the serpent beguiled or enticed me.

Notice, God never asked the serpent his motives. This is because the serpent represents the rational minds of humanity. If the serpent or the Devil were an entity unto itself, it would have made sense to find out its intentions. God is omniscience. He does not need to ask anything. This story is for our benefit. The fact that God does not question the serpent is additional proof that the Devil is not a separate life form.

Now we see God handing out punishments. In actuality, these are only the after effects of the rebellion. God is not like man. He does not get angry over every little thing we do wrong. By personifying Him, it helps us to understand our relationship and the spiritual realities that pertain to us.

When God speaks to the serpent, there is a duality between the physical and spiritual punishments. Serpents originally had four legs and later lost them and began to slither around. The writer draws these types of analogies to keep the continuity of the legend narrative. The real consequence is the enmity between the Woman, the serpent and their respective seeds.

We know the serpent represents the human rational mind. What is its seed? The seed of the mind, in the Bible represents the world or the flesh. The Woman we know is the Holy City, her seed of course refers ultimately to Jesus Christ the last Adam. If we wanted to be exact, the Woman gives birth to Jerusalem and she gives birth to the Messiah. The world and the people of God (the Woman) have always had hostility for as long as anyone can remember. This however is the starting point.

Couched in this legend is the Bible's first prophecy, "it shall bruise (some translations say crush) your head and you will bruise his heel." How does Christ bruise or crush the serpent's head?

> *Daniel 2:44 And in the days of these kings shall the **God of heaven set up a kingdom**, which shall never be destroyed: and the kingdom shall not be left to other people, but **it shall break in pieces and consume all these kingdoms**, and it shall stand for ever.*

Jesus came in His first Advent and setup the Kingdom of God. This Kingdom will break into pieces (crush) and consume every kingdom of the world (serpent's seed). Where is the Kingdom of God? The book of St. Luke declares the Kingdom of God is within us.[70] This is important to remember in reference to the Garden of Eden.

There is normally a duality in scriptures connected to Christ. Since, He is second in the Godhead. The number two signifies Him in scriptures.

So, how else does Christ bruise or crush the serpent's head? Where do we see the serpent? He is in the garden or the mind of humanity. He is associated to the tree of Knowledge of Good and Evil. Look at his titles. He is the accuser of the brethren, the adversary, the enemy and the dragon. In the book of Job, we see him debating God about the sincerity of Job's faith.

These images show us people and their collective thoughts. The accuser is always there whenever you try to improve or change yourself. These are your inner thoughts or voice accusing you. Jesus came to set us free from the inner conflict. This is what the picture of Christ crushing the head is conveying. Our head is the one that needs to be overcome (crushed).

> *Romans 12:2 And be not conformed to this world: but **be ye transformed by the renewing of your mind**, that ye may prove what is that good, and acceptable, and perfect, will of God.*

How exactly do we renew our minds? The most powerful tool available does this for us, the Word. It is sharper than any two-edged sword and the power of God unto salvation. All of that is nice to know, but how does the Word renew our minds? The process works by faith. The apostle Paul declares, "Faith comes by hearing the Word of God."[71] In order to explain this fully, I will borrow some text from "How to Live the Abundant Life."

"We commonly divide the mind into two parts, the conscious and the subconscious. Beliefs are formed in the conscious mind and if the belief is strong enough or repeated enough then it will be reproduced in the subconscious mind (This is not meant to be a comprehensive explanation on how the subconscious works).

Once a belief is moved into the subconscious it becomes stronger. The belief at this point changes to a conviction. This is also how faith works. Reading the Word of God and agreeing with it, is not faith but belief. Only after what we believe moves into our subconscious, does it become true faith.

Neuroscientists have shown that the conscious mind provides 5% or less of our cognitive (conscious) activity while we are awake. That means most of our decisions, actions, emotions and behavior depend on the 95% of brain activity that is stored in our subconscious. So how do we get things into our subconscious mind?

Two methods naturally come to mind. The first is repetition and the second is visualization. This is certainly not an exhaustive list, but these techniques are familiar to most people.

> *Romans 10:17 So then **faith cometh by hearing**, and hearing by the word of God.*

Notice faith comes through hearing, not from having heard. Adding the "ing" to the word "hear" gives it a present continuous tense. This implies repetition. God expects us to hear His Word on a continual basis. Hearing with the outer ear comes primarily comes from listening to voice of others. Whereas, hearing with the inner ear requires that we hear our voice speak the Word. Hearing through the inner ear is a more potent method when it comes to the affecting the subconscious.

> *Joshua 1:8* ***This book of the law shall not depart out of thy mouth;*** *but* ***thou shalt meditate therein day and night****, that thou mayest observe to do according to all that is written therein: for then thou shalt make thy way prosperous, and then thou shalt have good success.*

God instructs Joshua not to let the law depart from his mouth. Notice, the Lord did not specify his hands, eyes or his heart (mind), only his mouth. Therefore, God wanted Joshua to speak the Law from his own lips. This would automatically cause him to hear it with his inner ear and affect his subconscious.

Next, God told Joshua to meditate on the Law day and night, in order to become prosperous and successful. In other words, Joshua was supposed to focus his thoughts on the Word of God and to ponder over it. Pondering over the promises of God means to see it in your mind's eye, so to speak. This implies visualization of God's promises.

Clearly, God intends for us to use both repetition and visualization in order to change our conscious beliefs into true faith. Real faith operates from our subconscious, not the conscious realm.

> *Psalms 119:11* ***Thy word have I hid in mine heart****, that I might not sin against thee.*

Generally, when the Bible refers to the heart of a person, it is referring to the subconscious mind. So, we must place the Word in our subconscious, in order not to sin against God." [72]

By filling our minds with the Word of Faith, we can silence the accuser in our minds. The Bible exhorts us to change our speech from I cannot do anything right, to, "I can do all things through Christ that strengthens me."[73] Whatever the need, doubt or problem, there is a Word that will combat it. This is how Christ, who is the Word become flesh, bruised the head of the serpent (our subconscious).

Genesis 3:16 Unto the woman he said, I will greatly multiply thy sorrow and thy conception; in sorrow thou shalt bring forth children; and thy desire shall be to thy husband, and he shall rule over thee.

Just like with the serpent, there are physical references relating to a female and the more important spiritual meaning behind them. Physically, women have had difficulty during conception because the increased brain size of humans means bigger heads. Ladies, need I say more?

On the spiritual side, the Woman is the Holy City, but a municipality cannot experience physical pain. Again, this refers to the people of God, the citizens of the city. Look at Israel as an example. When Egypt birthed Israel this process was painful. It took four hundred years of slavery and ten plagues be delivered from their birth pangs.

Who is the husband that will rule over God's people (the Woman)? The husband is Adam of course. Adam is not a formal name, but the Hebrew word for humans. Therefore, man (generic use) will rule over God's people and their desire will be towards him or her.

This relates to religion, because God's people are spread out everywhere, in various religions. What this verse is telling us, since the Woman listened to their inner voice (voice of humanity) over God. They will continually desire this voice. In other words, people will look for leaders and trust in them over the Lord. If this was not the case, most of the religions today could never have the doctrines they espouse. To compound this fact, once you are a member, it is almost heresy to go against or even question any (man-made) practices.

Even in all of this, God's people were supposed to be free when the last Adam appeared. However, regrettably many are still in bondage. Today, many people of God (the Woman) still desire their first husband to rule over them. This is indeed a sad state of affairs.

Genesis 3:17 And unto Adam he said, Because thou hast hearkened unto the voice of thy wife, and hast eaten of the tree, of which I commanded thee, saying, Thou shalt not eat of it: cursed is the ground for thy sake; in sorrow shalt thou eat of it all the days of thy life;
Genesis 3:18 Thorns also and thistles shall it bring forth to thee; and thou shalt eat the herb of the field;
Genesis 3:19 In the sweat of thy face shalt thou eat bread, till thou return unto the ground; for out of it wast thou taken: for dust thou art, and unto dust shalt thou return.

Here we finally get to Adam (male and female) and their consequences. The physical aspect is hard work. Now we will severely lack what we really need, food.

Work has become misery and then we die. Wow, that is depressing. Job put it like this, "A man that is born of a woman is of few days, and full of trouble."[74] So, what is the point of living? God has already in His infinite love towards us, provided a remedy for our sins. He enacted various covenants with humanity, until the time was right and the Messiah came. The repercussions from the tree of Knowledge of Good and Evil are dire, but the Lord provides us with hope.

What Adam reaped not only affected them, but it disturbed the food sources of all creation. This makes sense we you realize man and woman were commissioned by the Lord, to be the gods of this world. Consequently, what impacts them, will be felt by everything under them.

On the spiritual side because Adam listened to the people of the Holy City, the repercussions of their actions cursed the ground. Now in sorrow they shall eat of it all the days of their lives. The Hebrew word for ground is "Adama" which is very close to the word for man. Earlier, we saw the two trees in the garden were actually the hemispheres of the brain. Trees are rooted in the ground. Therefore, the ground represents the mind of Adam. The ground will not bring forth as it should due to thorns and thistles. In other words, we as individuals will not be as spiritually fruitful as we should. This relates to faith, not intellect.

The word ground in the Bible is symbolic of the heart (Jeremiah 4:3, Hosea 10:12). I believe the parable of the Sower is best illustration of Adam's punishment in action.

> *Matthew 13:18 Hear ye therefore the parable of the sower.*
> *Matthew 13:19* **When any one heareth the word** *of the kingdom,* **and understandeth it not***, then cometh the wicked one, and* **catcheth away that which was sown in his heart***. This is he which received seed by the way side.*
> *Matthew 13:20 But he that received the seed into stony places, the same is* **he that heareth the word, and anon with joy receiveth it;**

Matthew 13:21 **Yet hath he not root in himself,** *but dureth for a while: for when tribulation or persecution ariseth because of the word, by and by he is offended.*
Matthew 13:22 **He also that received seed among the thorns** *is he that heareth the word; and* **the care of this world, and the deceitfulness of riches, choke the word,** *and he becometh unfruitful.*
Matthew 13:23 But **he that received seed into the good ground is he that heareth the word, and understandeth it;** *which also beareth fruit, and bringeth forth, some an hundredfold, some sixty, some thirty.*

Because humans hearkened (listened) to the voice of the Woman, over God, the ground of their hearts became hardened (cursed). Now we find it difficult to produce what we need, spiritually. Jesus plainly tells us the thorns (curse) are the cares of life and deceitfulness of riches.

Another practical example of how eating from the tree of knowledge of good and evil has affected us, is given by the apostle Paul.

Romans 7:15 And I have no clear knowledge of what I am doing, for that which I have a mind to do, I do not, but what I have hate for, that I do.
Romans 7:16 But, if I do that which I have no mind to do, **I am in agreement with the law that the law is good.**
Romans 7:17 So it is no longer I who do it, but the sin living in me.
Romans 7:18 For I am conscious that in me, that is, in my flesh, there is nothing good: I have the mind but not the power to do what is right.
Romans 7:19 **For the good which I have a mind to**

> **do, I do not: but the evil which I have no mind to do, that I do.**
> Romans 7:20 But if I do what I have no mind to do, it is no longer I who do it, but the sin living in me.
> Romans 7:21 So I see a law that, though **I have a mind to do good, evil is present in me.**

In these verses, we can clearly see the ground that is cursed is the mind of humans. We can also see how greatly this curse has affected us. Thankfully, Christ has redeemed us from the curse and we are now free.

> Galatians 3:13 **Christ hath redeemed us** from the curse of the law, **being made a curse for us**: for it is written, Cursed is every one that hangeth on a tree:

Salvation is instantaneous. However, our minds renew only as we work at it. For that reason, we may be saved for a long time, but our minds could remain unchanged. In other words, salvation does not equal transformation.

The process of faith was natural and easy to us, but the tree of Knowledge of Good and Evil has clogged its development. We believe the promises of God with our conscious mind, but our subconscious challenges with negative images and messages (thorns and thistles).

Christ the last Adam declares by faith we can have not only our needs met, but also our desires.

> Mark 11:23 For verily I say unto you, **That whosoever shall say unto this mountain, Be thou removed, and be thou cast into the sea; and shall not doubt in his heart,** but shall believe that those things which he saith shall come to pass; **he shall have whatsoever he saith.**

> *Mark 11:24* ***Therefore I say unto you, What things soever ye desire, when ye pray, believe that ye receive them, and ye shall have them.***

How many people can say they can make this verse work for them, even half of the time? Why is this, the case? Is Jesus selling us a bill of goods? Our minds (subconscious) must be in agreement with our confession (conscious mind). The law of faith only works in conjunction with the law of agreement.

> *James 1:6* But ***let him ask in faith, nothing wavering****. For he that wavereth is like a wave of the sea driven with the wind and tossed.*
> *James 1:7* For ***let not that man think that he shall receive any thing of the Lord.***
> *James 1:8* ***A double minded man is unstable in all his ways.***

To be double-minded means you believe one thing consciously, but there is conflict in your subconscious. You may not even be aware of the conflict. The bottom line, it takes work to reprogram the subconscious mind. Transformation happens brick by brick, so to speak. The first step is identifying the conflict. Then the real work begins. Unfortunately, this is what it means to have the ground (mind) cursed.

The last part of Genesis 3:19, talks about returning to the dust. The implication is Adam was not meant to die and death came about through the fall. However, men and women died before God placed Adam in the Eden. Therefore, physical death cannot be the issue.

God is the source of all life. Therefore, separation from God means death and this is what the writer is implying.

Once God fused His Spirit with our frame (dust), the result was an immortal soul. At the point of physical death, the soul of humans is supposed to return to God. This is life eternal. In this verse, we have Adam returning to the dust.

The pictorial illustration is humanity going down to the grave, instead of up with God. This is death, in a spiritual sense. The soul never dies. We do not just cease to exist. But we have either everlasting life or eternal damnation. The purpose of the last Adam is to restore us, to life eternal.

Genesis 3:20 And Adam called his wife's name Eve; because she was the mother of all living.
Genesis 3:21 Unto Adam also and to his wife did the LORD God make coats of skins, and clothed them.
Genesis 3:22 And the LORD God said, Behold, the man is become as one of us, to know good and evil: and now, lest he put forth his hand, and take also of the tree of life, and eat, and live for ever:
Genesis 3:23 Therefore the LORD God sent him forth from the garden of Eden, to till the ground from whence he was taken.
Genesis 3:24 So he drove out the man; and he placed at the east of the garden of Eden Cherubims, and a flaming sword which turned every way, to keep the way of the tree of life.

Here we see Adam both male and female naming the city. They called the name of the place, Eve. This should be the first human civilization. Now, the title "mother of all living", makes perfect sense. The relationship between Eve and Eden is akin to Jerusalem and Israel.

There are so many allusions that tell us Adam and Eve are not the first couple on earth, it is hard to ignore.

Indicators Adam and Eve were not alone
1. Adam named the animals – meaning language was created already
2. Adam (male and female) is commanded to be fruitful and multiply
3. Eve is called the mother of all living
4. Cain fears people will find and kill him, so God put a mark upon him (Gen 4:14-15)

Next, we see the Lord making skins for Adam and his wife, which means the whole city. We can take two approaches to understanding this passage. Either, God made animal skins for the people to wear. Alternatively, He clothed them with human flesh. The first option would entail a great deal of animal killing. This seems to go against the lesson of the tree of knowledge. Therefore, we have God making Adam and his wife mortals. This would be in keeping with the mythological style of writing of the day.

Adam and the city of Eve are the gods of the earth, by design. They were intended to draw the other hominids to God, just as Israel was supposed to do with the Gentile nations. The city of Eve was the Lord's chosen people. They were the sons and daughters of God. As a result, when they fell in the garden, they became mortals. This of course is only a literary allusion, pointing to their spiritual status.

The shortening of Adam and his descendants lifespans, further highlights their loss of status. Gradually through the generations, the sons of God began to live shorter lives, until we get to God ordained a limit of 120 years.[75] God prevented access to the tree of life and living forever.

Again, we see this allusion in Genesis chapter six, when it talks about the sons of God marrying the daughters of men.

Their offspring became giants and men of great renown. When all of the sons of God finally died, meaning their lifespans came into the range of 120 years, we see their official status changed from sons to servants of God. This is the true fall of man (male and female). We have gone from gods to mere mortals.

> *Leviticus 25:55* ***For unto me the children of Israel are servants; they are my servants*** *whom I brought forth out of the land of Egypt: I am the LORD your God.*

The irony is the city of Eve (Woman) ate the forbidden fruit with the intention of becoming like God. Yet, they were already like Him, created in His image and likeness. Their action resulted in them losing sonship and becoming God's servants. But, thankfully Christ the last Adam has regained this status for us and now we are once again the sons of God.

Through Christ, we have regained access to the tree of life. This is a future occurrence and is actually the trees of life. I will explain. Adam could only eat the forbidden fruit by disobeying the commandment of God. Conversely, he could only eat from the tree of life by obeying the Word of the Lord. Jesus is called the "Bread of Life" and through Him, we have the promise of eternal life. I said promise because nothing is final until Judgment, when the Lord opens the "Book of Life." If your name is inside, then you will have full access to the trees of life in New Jerusalem. In the new Holy City, there are two trees of life, which correspond to the number of Christ in the Godhead. Jesus the long awaited Messiah is the key to it all.

Today, we eat the bread of life just as Adam did with the tree of life, through obedience to the Word of God. The reference to Jesus being the bread of life, relates to the manna Israel received in the wilderness. When the tribes got to the Promised Land, the manna stopped. It was temporary until they reached the Holy Land.

Likewise, Christ the bread of life is our manna, until we reach New Jerusalem. Once we are in the new Holy City, there will be a tree of life on both sides of the river. The tree of knowledge of Good and Evil will no longer exist, because perfect knowledge will eradicate it.

Remember, I said earlier this is why the scriptures construct a day as the evening and the morning. We start in darkness and end in the light. In the next age, New Jerusalem there will be only light.

Knowledge of Good and Evil has plunged humans into darkness. There is no light apart from God. We started to believe our minds. Our intellect became our gods and it ruled us. God's knowledge is analogous to light and human knowledge equates to darkness. Light overpowers and removes darkness. Perfect knowledge is the glory of God.

After Adam and the city of Eve descend to mortality, they lose access to the garden. Now they must till the ground and Cherubim protect the tree of Life. In the natural, this most likely correlates to the exodus of humanity from Africa over a million years ago. This forcing out probably was due to food shortages or some climatic condition. Either of these would be a direct consequence of the fall. Now humans have to work hard to get what they need to survive.

On the spiritual side, how can humanity be removed from the garden? Remember, we never stated the purpose of the garden. I said the physical location is the brain, but besides that what is it? The garden of God is the Most Holy Place or the Holiest of Holies. It is the place where humanity communes or meets with God.

How do we know the garden is the Most Holy Place? Cherubim, plural are set up over the gate to protect the tree of Life. They have flaming swords, which imply any unlawful entry will result in death. In the Holies of Holies, over the Ark of the Covenant, there are two cherubs or cherubim (plural of cherub). What is in the Ark? It contains the stone tables of Moses (Law), which is the Word of Life. If anyone, but the High Priest comes inside, they immediately fall dead. The High Priest goes in once a year to offer atonement. If he enters any other time or enters in an improper manner, he too will die. He wears a bell when entering, so the other priest will know he is still alive by its ringing. The garden is where God would come to talk to Adam and the Most Holy Place is where God abides to speak with the High Priest. If the garden is the Most Holy Place, then where is the rest of the tabernacle?

1 Corinthians 3:16 **Know ye not that ye are the temple of God**, *and that the Spirit of* **God dwelleth in you**?

From the very beginning of time, this was true. We were and are God's temple, His dwelling place. If our minds are the garden, then practically speaking we cannot be kicked out of it.

This removal means the way to God became suppressed or lost. We could no longer see the truth and our carnal minds became our gods. This is spiritual blindness. The impairment of spiritual vision led us to believe the Lord was far from us. When in actuality He was within. But, as a man thinks, so he is.[76] Therefore, our belief became our reality.

We became detached from God, resulting in spiritual death. Due to our blindness, we started searching for God outside of ourselves. We formed religions, rituals and rules, in order to earn the Lord's favor. Since we sinned and fell from grace, we concluded, God must be angry with us. To combat this we performed sacrifices, in order to appease Him.

How could our meager actions ever placate the Almighty? Consequently, we imagined when disaster happened it was because He was displeased. The sun naturally became God because it was bright and powerful. However, droughts came and we needed rain. Consequently, we thought there must be another god of rain and we have displeased him by honoring the sun too much. For everything that went wrong there emerged a new god. Now, there were gods everywhere and they all needed to be appeased.

God meets us where we are. This is a truism. If we are the sons of God, then naturally He is our Father. As such, He is not willing for His children suffer. Fittingly, He intervened. The Creator left His Sabbath and went back to work. This time it was for the redemption and salvation of humanity. He began to initiate covenants with us. The covenants and mighty acts of the Lord revealed that He alone, was the one and true God. His laws showed us how to please and honor Him.

Finally, His Son told us how much God loves us and that He will never leave or forsake us. The last Adam opened up salvation for all people.

Jesus did not initiate a covenant with us. In form, a *covenant* is an agreement between two or more people and involves promises on the part of one or more parties. A covenant ends when one of the parties dies. Since God cannot die, the covenant is over upon our death. Jesus came to establish a covenant that could not be broken, even at death.

> *Ezekiel 37:26 Moreover* ***I will make a covenant of peace with them; it shall be an everlasting covenant with them: and I*** *will place them, and multiply them, and* ***will set my sanctuary in the midst of them for evermore.***

If all covenants terminate at death and all men die, how can Christ accomplish this feat? Instead of a covenant, Jesus formed a testament. A testament begins after the testator dies and does not end, but must be fulfilled. It is analogous to an irrevocable trust. Hence, death terminates covenants, but initiates testaments. This is another reason Jesus had to come in the flesh.

Now that the last Adam's work is over, He is back with the Father. The work of redemption is complete. It is once again, the Sabbath. The Father has placed us in Christ, for one purpose, rest. How can we rest, when there is so much work to do? Our permanent rest is in New Jerusalem. Israel prefigured our rest in Christ, in the wilderness.

I know you are saying, how was that rest? Marching around in the hot sun for 40 years, some rest. Did Israel have to till the ground during this time? Did they have to get part-time jobs to support their families? Did they starve to death? Were they naked because they could not buy new clothes? In all of these things, God provided. That is rest.

In Egypt, they were slaves. The Lord caused the Egyptians to give them riches, before the exodus. They embarked on a journey to the Promised Land and all they had to do was trust in their God. The Church is in the same situation now. God has promised to provide for our every need and more. We are simply on a journey to the Promise Land.

What about testifying and reaching others? The greatest testimony we will ever have is proving the Word of God, by our lives, not our lips. We have come full circle. Christ has done what the first Adam could not. Once again, God dwells within us. We have paradise within our grasps. Just like Adam, we have a choice to make. Which tree will I eat from today?

The Serpent Revisited

We left off in Genesis chapter three with the assumption the serpent represented the rationale human mind. This of course flies in the face of traditional religious thinking and teaching. We know that Satan is real and he is the enemy of God and all of creation. Anything else is almost blasphemy.

Mainstream Judaism contains no overt concept of a devil. However, Christianity and Islam regard the Devil as a rebellious fallen angel that tempts humans to sin. Modern Christian thought usually portrays God and the Devil fighting over the souls of humanity. The Devil leads other fallen angels, commonly known as demons, in a campaign to entice people into sin and ultimately into Hell.

First, is the Devil a fallen angelic being? There are no direct scriptures stating the origin of Satan. The book of Isaiah refers to Lucifer, another name commonly given to the Devil.

> *Isaiah 14:12* ***How art thou fallen from heaven, O Lucifer, son of the morning!*** *how art thou cut down to the ground, which didst weaken the nations!*
> *Isaiah 14:13* ***For thou hast said in thine heart, I will ascend into heaven, I will exalt my throne above the stars of God:*** *I will sit also upon the mount of the congregation, in the sides of the north:*
> *Isaiah 14:14 I will ascend above the heights of the clouds;* ***I will be like the most High.***
> *Isaiah 14:15 Yet thou shalt be brought down to hell, to the sides of the pit.*

Isaiah 14:16 They that see thee shall narrowly look upon thee, and consider thee, saying, **Is this the man that made the earth to tremble, that did shake kingdoms;**

In verse four of Isaiah chapter fourteen it states, this is a proverb (parable). Lucifer means light bearer or brilliant star. The term refers to the King of Babylon, not Satan. The proverb is allegoric in form, alluding to the sin of the Woman in the Garden of Eden. Nevertheless, verse sixteen clearly states, Lucifer is a man not an angelic being.

Next, we will look at the book of Ezekiel and the King of Tyre. These verses of scripture commonly connect us to the Devil.

Ezekiel 28:1 The word of the LORD came again unto me, saying,
Ezekiel 28:2 Son of man, **say unto the prince of Tyrus***, Thus saith the Lord GOD;* **Because thine heart is lifted up, and thou hast said, I am a God,** *I sit in the seat of God, in the midst of the seas;* **yet thou art a man, and not God***, though thou set thine heart as the heart of God:*

Ezekiel 28:12 **Son of man, take up a lamentation upon the king of Tyrus [Tyre]***, and say unto him, Thus saith the Lord GOD; Thou sealest up the sum, full of wisdom, and perfect in beauty.*
Ezekiel 28:13 **Thou hast been in Eden the garden of God***; every precious stone was thy covering, the sardius, topaz, and the diamond, the beryl, the onyx, and the jasper, the sapphire, the emerald, and the carbuncle, and gold: the workmanship of thy tabrets and of thy pipes was prepared in thee in the day that thou wast created.*

Ezekiel 28:14 **Thou art the anointed cherub that covereth**; *and I have set thee so: thou wast upon the holy mountain of God; thou hast walked up and down in the midst of the stones of fire.*

Ezekiel 28:15 **Thou wast perfect in thy ways from the day that thou wast created, till iniquity was found in thee.**

Ezekiel 28:16 By the multitude of thy merchandise they have filled the midst of thee with violence, and thou hast sinned: therefore I will cast thee as profane out of the mountain of God: and I will destroy thee, O covering cherub, from the midst of the stones of fire.

Ezekiel 28:17 **Thine heart was lifted up because of thy beauty, thou hast corrupted thy wisdom by reason of thy brightness: I will cast thee to the ground**, *I will lay thee before kings, that they may behold thee.*

Ezekiel 28:18 Thou hast defiled thy sanctuaries by the multitude of thine iniquities, by the iniquity of thy traffick; therefore will I bring forth a fire from the midst of thee, it shall devour thee, and I will bring thee to ashes upon the earth in the sight of all them that behold thee.

Ezekiel 28:19 **All they that know thee among the people shall be astonished at thee: thou shalt be a terror, and never shalt thou be any more.**

Right in the first verse of the chapter the prophet states, "You are a man and not God." This statement should be the decisive factor in determining whom Ezekiel is referring. In Isaiah, we looked at a proverb. This text is a lamentation or an epitaph to the King of Trye. Again, we have an allegory referring to the Garden of Eden, the Most Holy Place or Mount Zion. These are all holy places where God communes with humanity.

The references to walking in the midst of fiery stones appears to parallel the pagan myths of sacred stones, which were purportedly endowed with life. The king was covered or clothed with precious stones, signifying he was to be a wall of defense to Israel.[77] This was in the form a treaty between Israel and Tyre.[78] The King of Tyre being the anointed covering cherub is another allusion to his role of protector over the people of God (Jerusalem, specifically the Holiest of Holies).

> *1 Peter 2:4 As you come to him, the living Stone— rejected by men but chosen by God and precious to him—*
> *1 Peter 2:5 **you also, like living stones**, are being built into a spiritual house to be **a holy priesthood**, offering spiritual sacrifices acceptable to God through Jesus Christ.*

The apostle Peter declares, the people of God are living stones. This is yet another reference to the pagan worship of sacred, life giving stones. This time Christ is the true living Stone and through Him, we receive life and become sacred stones of the spiritual house of God (aka temple of God).

In the end, Ezekiel tells us the King falls (was cast) to the ground or earth. This is analogous to Adam's punishment of returning to the earth. In both cases, God was dealing with the sin of humans not angelic beings.

In verse nineteen the prophet states, the people who know the king will be astonished and he will be no more. If these verses pertain to Satan, when did anyone see him destroyed? Most people believe he is alive and well. Ezekiel said God would reduce him to ashes on the earth, in front of everyone. Conversely, the Devil has not been burned to cinders on earth, but instead the book of Revelation states, he will be thrown into the lake of fire in the future.

Both Isaiah and Ezekiel use mythological references to the Garden of Eden, in order to highlight we are still guilty of committing the sin as Adam. We are in fact repeating the sins of our father. There is no biblical text confirming the heavenly origins of the Devil or any angelic connection to him.

We should also look at Revelation to see what it has to say about the matter of Satan, since it links four different names to the same entity.

> *Revelation 12:9* **And the great dragon was cast out, that old serpent, called the Devil, and Satan**, *which deceiveth the whole world: he was cast out into the earth, and his angels were cast out with him.*

Revelation chapter twelve identifies the great dragon of the book, as the same entity called the old serpent, the Devil and Satan. Genesis and Revelation are like the bookends of the Bible. One tells of the beginnings of things and the other a summation. Chapter 12 is a synopsis or clarification of the figure called the Devil.

In chapter 12, John sees two wonders appearing in heaven. We have two mysteries to solve. This indicates the true meaning is buried somewhere in scripture. The first mystery is a Woman about to give birth and the second is a great dragon threatening her child. Since the dragon is also the old serpent, the confrontation with the woman and her child is familiar.

> *Genesis 3:15 And **I will put enmity between thee and the woman, and between thy seed and her seed**; it shall bruise thy head, and thou shalt bruise his heel.*

The Woman in Revelation is the Holy City, Jerusalem. The man-child who will rule all the nations with an iron scepter is Christ.[79] God snatches the child up to heaven and His throne. The signs occurred in heaven, but when the man-child is born, he ascends to God. This indicates the birth was actually on earth.

What is happening here is we are viewing the earthly events from a heavenly perspective. In other words, this is the spiritual view of what took place during the birth of Christ. For instance, the dragon attempts to devour the child the moment he was born. This is the heavenly perspective. On earth, Herod killed all of the children two years old and younger, in Bethlehem and its coast in order to stop the King of the Jews from coming. The dragon is merely a spiritual representation of Herod, in this particular instance.

Genesis 3:15 indicates the seed of the Woman (Christ) will bruise or crush the head of the serpent. Oddly, the child in Revelation disappears shortly after birth and is uninvolved in the expulsion of the dragon from heaven. What is really going on and why is Christ not involved, since He is the seed of the Woman?

Another narrative fills in the blanks. Unfortunately, there is no intuitive link and consequently, it is never associated to Revelation. The story of Ishmael and Isaac shows why Christ seems disconnected to the conflict with the dragon.

*Genesis 21:8 And the child grew, and was weaned: and **Abraham made a great feast the same day that Isaac was weaned.***

*Genesis 21:9 **And Sarah saw the son of Hagar the Egyptian**, which she had born unto Abraham, **mocking**.*

*Genesis 21:10 **Wherefore she said unto Abraham, Cast out this bondwoman and her son: for the son of this bondwoman shall not be heir with my son**, even with Isaac.*

The apostle Paul states in Galatians chapter four, the son of the bondwoman (Hagar) was born after the flesh, but the son of the freewoman (Sarah) was by promise. He goes on to say, this is an allegory of two covenants. Paul tells us Hagar represents physical Jerusalem and Sarah symbolizes New Jerusalem, which is above (spiritual).

Next, he states, just as the son of the flesh (Ishmael) persecuted the son born after the spirit (Isaac), so it still goes on today. Using Paul's analogy it becomes clear, Adam embodies Ishmael and Jesus represents Isaac.

In the account of Ishmael and Isaac, there was a great feast when Sarah weaned Isaac. Sarah saw Ishmael mocking Isaac and this caused Hagar and her son to be cast out. How does this relate to Christ? During the great feast of unleavened bread (Passover), the seed of the flesh mocked Jesus.

*St. Matthew 27:29 And when they had platted a crown of thorns, they put it upon his head, and a reed in his right hand: and **they bowed the knee before him, and mocked him, saying, Hail, King of the Jews!***

> *St. Matthew 27:39* **And they that passed by reviled him***, wagging their heads,*
> *St. Matthew 27:40* *And* **saying***,* **Thou that destroyest the temple, and buildest it in three days, save thyself.** *If thou be the Son of God, come down from the cross.*
> *St. Matthew 27:41* **Likewise also the chief priests mocking him, with the scribes and elders, said,**
> *St. Matthew 27:42* **He saved others; himself he cannot save.** *If he be the King of Israel,* **let him now come down from the cross, and we will believe him.**

The resurrection of Christ is the real cause of the dragon's displacement. The book of Luke chapter three declares Adam is the "Son of God." This term is exclusive to Adam and Jesus in the Bible. Everywhere else, the term changes to "Sons of God" or "a son of God" for believers. As the son of God, Adam had dominion over the earth and access to heaven. All of this was his, by inheritance. The Lord never took these rights away from Adam. This is why we see Satan showing up with the sons of God in the book of Job.

Going back to Revelation 12, we can now see why Christ is not depicted crushing the head of the serpent. It was the birth of Isaac and subsequent feast, which caused Ishmael to be cast out. Likewise, Christ is the son of promise and His birth caused the dragon to lose his place. This was necessary because as the son of God, Adam inherits the throne. Paul states in 1 Corinthians 15:50, "flesh and blood cannot inherit the Kingdom of God; neither can corruption inherit incorruption." This is why the man-child ascended to God and His throne. He has inherited it by birthright, as the son of promise.

Now we can see why all of the names of the Devil, are listed in Revelation. God wants it to be clear. There is no rebellious fallen angel bent on causing us to sin and go to hell. When we view the devil in scripture, it is really a depiction of the fallen state of man.

Who are the angels the dragon dragged down to the earth? Since the dragon or serpent represents our Adamic nature (our flesh). Then demons are the seed of the serpent, mentioned in Genesis 3. In scripture, they are also known as, the world, Gentiles, heathen, sinners and unbelievers.

What were the demons Jesus cast out of people? These are infirmities and mental illnesses in the people healed by Christ. During the time of Christ, people believed demons caused these things. By healing them, Jesus showed the power of God is greater than any demon real or imagined.

I know what you are thinking. Clearly, demons possessed the man who said his name was Legion. Notice, after Jesus commanded the demons to leave, the man was clothed in his right mind. This means with the demons he was not in his right mind. This man most likely suffered from schizophrenia. Unfortunately, no one in ancient times understood this mental disorder. Therefore, demon possession was the common diagnosis.

In regards to Satan, think about this. In the book of Revelation everyone must stand before God and be judged for their deeds, good or bad. However, Satan is cast into the lake of fire, but he is never judged. If he were a fallen angel, would God be right in not judging him? After all, we have to answer for everything we have done. Why would the Devil be exempt?

There are too many scriptures about the Devil to address all of them individually. I hope that you are convinced. Either way, I encourage you to do your own research.

Satan is a big part of religion. It is hard to eliminate him. It is normal to have nagging doubts and questions. For instance, who tempted Jesus in the wilderness?

Just like Eve in the garden, the Devil was in His mind. To me it feels a lot better to imagine Christ struggling with the same thoughts I do, than squaring off with some supernatural figure on a mountain. Now, His temptations seem real, instead of epic.

How could Jesus be tempted in all points like me, but without sin, [80] if his thoughts were always holy and pure? We can take comfort knowing the only Devil we need to defeat is our mind. The enemy is only defeated, as we renew our minds. If we do not fill our minds (subconscious) with faith, we will be sons of God, living like servants.

The dissolution of the Devil will have a definite impact of our and the Church's theology. Fighting the Devil has become a lucrative industry. Now, there is no longer anyone to blame for anything, other than ourselves. Wow. Finally, we can stop talking about Satan and focus on the real enemy.

What is our warfare strategy now? I echo the words of Paul, "Let this mind be in you, which was also in Christ Jesus."[81]

Out of Eden

Genesis 4:1 And Adam knew Eve his wife; and she conceived, and bare Cain, and said, I have gotten a man from the LORD.
Genesis 4:2 And she again bare his brother Abel. And Abel was a keeper of sheep, but Cain was a tiller of the ground.
Genesis 4:3 And in process of time it came to pass, that Cain brought of the fruit of the ground an offering unto the LORD.
Genesis 4:4 And Abel, he also brought of the firstlings of his flock and of the fat thereof. And the LORD had respect unto Abel and to his offering:
Genesis 4:5 But unto Cain and to his offering he had not respect. And Cain was very wroth, and his countenance fell.
Genesis 4:6 And the LORD said unto Cain, Why art thou wroth? and why is thy countenance fallen?
Genesis 4:7 If thou doest well, shalt thou not be accepted? and if thou doest not well, sin lieth at the door. And unto thee *shall be* his desire, and thou shalt rule over him.
Genesis 4:8 And Cain talked with Abel his brother: and it came to pass, when they were in the field, that Cain rose up against Abel his brother, and slew him.

This portion of Adam's legend is just as full of analogies as the previous chapter. It is not just a simple story about two brothers. Why does God go through all of the trouble of hiding things? Humanity was not at the stage of maturity to handle ultimate truths in the beginning. To put it in biblical terms, it would be casting your pearls before swine.[82] Once we evolved or matured as a people, God could reveal His truth to us. Jesus Christ the last Adam was that truth.

Therefore, in the Old Testament spiritual truths concerning the Messiah are hidden or sealed. In contrast, Jesus Christ openly proclaims God's truth in the New Testament. We see this illustrated in the book of Revelation. The 7 Seals symbolize the Old Covenant, which is contrasted to 7 trumpets representing New Testament era. Seals denote concealment and trumpets epitomize proclaiming.

On the surface, Adam and Eve had two sons. The eldest killed the younger due to jealously. The fall of humanity relates directly to this story. Sealed in symbolism are the origin and effects of sin.

The Woman is enticed by the serpent and eats from the Tree of Knowledge. Later, Adam impregnates Eve and conceives Cain. In the course of time, Cain kills his brother Abel. In this story, we are detached from the characters. They are not us and we are not them. I have heard Christians complain about the naivety of Eve. This shows we do not readily associate ourselves to the narrative.

After Jesus' first Advent, the Bible proclaims the same truth previously sealed. The apostle James illuminates the Eden narrative in the New Testament.

> *James 1:13* **Let no man say when he is tempted, I am tempted of God**: *for God cannot be tempted with evil, neither tempteth he any man:*
> *James 1:14* **But every man is tempted, when he is drawn away of his own lust,** *and enticed.*

James 1:15 Then **when lust hath conceived, it bringeth forth sin: and sin, when it is finished, bringeth forth death.**

Now we can clearly see the symbolism of the fall. Temptation is never external. Our lust causes us sin, not the devil. Therefore, the serpent must be within us. Cain represents the sin of the Woman, born from lust. Her actions in the garden conceived him. This is why in the narrative, Adam only knows his wife after the fall. Since Cain symbolizes sin, it is natural that he brings them death.

As I stated earlier, death means separation from God, not ceasing to exist. Adam as our federal head or prototype gave us his nature by default. This is why Jesus had to come and replace him. The first Adam condemned all humanity to death (separation from God). The last Adam reunited everyone back to God (life eternal).

Continuing the narrative, although Cain represents sin, he chooses his own path as an individual. Cain and his brother Abel are depicted presenting offerings to God. Humankind is already performing acts of propitiation to God. This is an attempt to appease the Lord and avoid divine retribution. If Adam and Eve are the first couple on earth, where did these two brothers acquire this religious observance?

Cain tills the land like his father Adam. However, Abel has the occupation of a shepherd. We have gone from eating prohibited meat, to domesticating and herding animals, in only a few short verses. Obviously, for the sake of the story time is compressed.

Cain offers the produce of the field to God. Similarly, Abel offers the produce of his flock. The difference being Abel offers the firstlings or firstborn and Cain does not. The first-fruits imagery is very familiar to Israel. Cain did not offer his first and best to God. Consequently, he did not receive the Lord's favor, which is the whole point of the offering. Naturally, Cain is upset not to receive his desire. However, instead of directing his anger at God, he uses transference and makes his brother the object of his wrath.

God asks Cain, why are you angry? He goes on to say, if you do right, you will have favor. Conversely, if you choose to do wrong, sin is crouching at your door. This is our first introduction to the term "sin." In the garden, before the fall, sin was an alien concept. Whereas, after eating the forbidden fruit, it became necessary to introduce the term and assign a meaning to it.

Notice, instead of a serpent beguiling Cain, sin is crouching at his door. We see sin as a male figure that desires to have Cain. This is the beginning of the infamous Devil. We see the same figure of speech with Simon Peter, "Satan desires to have you, that he may sift you as wheat."[83] We can infer from their usage, the terms "sin" and "Satan" are interchangeable. Therefore, the Devil is merely the personification of sin.

Where does sin reside? It crouches at the door of our hearts. Remember, the heart is our subconscious mind. It is shown crouching to illustrate we will not see it coming. Indeed, we cannot see it, since it is part of us. This is obviously to our disadvantage.

The good news is we have the ability to rule over sin. Meaning we have control over our subconscious. God is saying you have power over sin. It does not have to dominate you.

1 Corinthians 10:13 **There hath no temptation taken you but such as is common to man**: *but God is faithful, who will not suffer you to be tempted above that ye are able;* **but will with the temptation also make a way to escape, that ye may be able to bear it.**

So much for the Devil made me do it. We sin because we choose to do it. The responsibility is ours and there is no one else to blame. I for one am tired of hearing about the exploits of the enemy. The Church has been preoccupied with the Devil, for far too long.

Before we move on, I think we should look at another parallel. Cain and Abel are a precursor to Ishmael and Isaac, respectively. Remember, Ishmael is the son of the bondwoman Hagar and Isaac is the son of promise. Although Ishmael is Abraham's son, since Hagar is his mother, he is also Abraham's slave. The name Cain in the Hebrew language means "Possession." A slave is the possession of the owner.

Abel's name is translated "Breath," in Hebrew. The breath of God is the Spirit of God. How does this relate to Abel being like Isaac, the son of promise? Ephesians 1:13 refers to the Holy Spirit as the Spirit of promise.

All of this is nice to know. But, what is the point of another reference to Ishmael and Isaac? This allusion answers a vital question. Why was it necessary for Ishmael to go away?

On the surface, it looks like a jealous reaction of Sarah, to Ishmael mocking Isaac. However, when we see the scenario played out with Cain and Abel, it is apparent separation is required. Due to the father's favor, Ishmael would eventually kill Isaac. We also saw this situation played out with Christ. When He was on the cross, people mocked and crucified him.

When we look at Cain and Abel, the son of promise is killed. However, in the story of Ishmael and Isaac, the son receives his inheritance. Both of these stories are necessary because although Jesus dies, he still receives the inheritance. Since, the stories contain what we believe to be real people; it is unthinkable for anyone to die and afterwards receive a birthright. Therefore, God retells the story with different outcomes. The ordering is of course important, but also apparent when we relate them to Christ.

Genesis 4:9 And the LORD said unto Cain, Where *is* Abel thy brother? And he said, I know not: *Am* I my brother's keeper?
Genesis 4:10 And he said, What hast thou done? the voice of thy brother's blood crieth unto me from the ground.
Genesis 4:11 And now *art* thou cursed from the earth, which hath opened her mouth to receive thy brother's blood from thy hand;
Genesis 4:12 When thou tillest the ground, it shall not henceforth yield unto thee her strength; a fugitive and a vagabond shalt thou be in the earth.
Genesis 4:13 And Cain said unto the LORD, My punishment *is* greater than I can bear.
Genesis 4:14 Behold, thou hast driven me out this day from the face of the earth; and from thy face shall I be hid; and I shall be a fugitive and a vagabond in the earth; and it shall come to pass, *that* every one that findeth me shall slay me.
Genesis 4:15 And the LORD said unto him, Therefore whosoever slayeth Cain, vengeance shall be taken on him sevenfold. And the LORD set a mark upon Cain, lest any finding him should kill him.

When the Lord speaks to Cain concerning the whereabouts of Abel, he fires back the infamous rhetorical question. Am I my brother's keeper? Think about this for a minute. If you just killed your brother and God asks you, where is he? Would you get insolent with the Almighty?

Obviously, this is a continuation of Adam's legend. It does not mean there was not an actual person named Cain. However, the narrative serves to convey spiritual truths. God is love. Everything we do must be motivated by it, because we are created in God's image. Therefore, yes we are our brother's keeper. Love compels this to be so.

The Lord said, "The voice of your brother's blood cries out to me from the ground." We can gather from the symbolic language, Cain buried Abel in order to hide his deed. Even though Abel is physically dead, his voice still reaches God. God is covertly telling us the soul lives even after the body is gone.

By killing Abel, Cain set the law of Reciprocity in motion. If you plant a seed, you reap a harvest. It is a one to many, relationship. This is why King David could say, "My cup runneth over." God intended for us to experience the good side of reciprocity. Unfortunately, Cain's action set him up to suffer an abundance of negative consequences.

He responded by saying, "My punishment is greater than I can bear." This is the human condition after the fall. God does not leave us to our own devices, but gives us mercy and grace.

Cain planted his dead brother in the ground and reaped death in the form of food shortages. Previously, Adam cursed the ground by his actions. Now, his seed compounds the situation so the earth will barely yield anything.

Cain must become a nomad in order to survive. This adds a wrinkle to the literal view of the narrative. He becomes a vagabond and a fugitive on the earth. This cannot be a punishment unless people normally live a stationary life. The writer describes Cain as a tiller of the ground, not a picker of fruit. The difference is significant.

When we think of Adam (male and female), we imagine them strolling through the garden casually picking fruit as they needed it. However, this was not the case with Cain he tilled the ground. This means, he cultivated the soil. His occupation was farming.

History has shown us that in the dawn of time, all humans were gatherers (like Adam). Humans then evolved into, hunter-gathers (more than likely scavenged animals) and gathered wild plants for their sustenance, until weapons were invented. However, farming did not develop until around 10,000 BC.[84]

Abel kept flocks of an unnamed animal. The first domesticated animals known in history are sheep and goats.[85] Shortly after the advent of farming, humans began to domesticate animals for food. Historically speaking there were over ten million humans on earth, when we learned how to domesticate animals and farm. Therefore, Cain could not possibly be the second male on earth.

> **Hesoid's Ages of Man**
> **(Greek poet, 8th-7th century B.C.)**
>
> I. Golden age (prehistory)
>   A. Age of the hunter-gatherer
>   B. Eden-like pre-agricultural
>
> II. Silver Age (8,000 B.C.)
>   A. Concept of work born
>   B. Symbolized by the "Yoke of Oxen"
>
> III. Bronze Age (3,500 B.C.)
>   A. Trade developed
>
> IV. Iron Age (1,500-600 B.C.)

Figure 8. History of Agricultural Development Lecture 1. Retrieved on 2 May 2013, from http://www.csustan.edu/agstudies/documents/AGST_3000/AgHistoryL1.ppt

Who or what does Cain represent? "The Ages of Man are the stages of human existence on the Earth according to Greek mythology. In the accounts that survive from ancient Greece and Rome, this degradation of the human condition over time is indicated symbolically with metals of successively decreasing value."[86] Adam exemplified the Golden Age, a time of innocence. Cain and Abel embody the Silver Age, the inception of organized labor. Therefore, Cain and Abel represent a new period where humans must work for a living.

Looking back at the narrative, if Cain is only the second male on the planet, why is he afraid of someone finding and killing him? Notice he does not say if my family finds me. This is another indication Adam and his family did not exist alone. Furthermore, God validated Cain's claim by setting a mark on him. If no one was around, but Cain's family what would be the point? God could have just spoken to Adam and that would be the end of it.

God does not explicitly reveal anything about the mark put upon Cain. What we do know is this mark symbolized His protection. We see this same imagery used with the nation of Israel in Ezekiel 9:4-6. The mark in the Old Testament is a precursor to the seal of God, which denotes the Holy Spirit. Oddly, instead of anger over Cain's actions, God shows him mercy. This is in line with the true nature of the Lord. When we deserve punishment, the Lord gives us grace.

Cain represents the human race in its fallen state and Abel prefigures Christ. Humanity crucified Jesus and deserved God's wrath. Like Cain, we could not withstand our punishment. Therefore, the Lord did not deal with us after our sins; neither did He reward us according to our iniquities.[87]

In order for us not to die, God set His mark upon us, just like Cain. On the day of Pentecost, the Lord sealed us with His Spirit and gave us eternal life. The same protection afforded to Cain is ours through Christ. Jesus said, "I beheld Satan as lighting fall from heaven. Behold, I give unto you power to tread on serpents and scorpions, and over all the power of the enemy: and nothing shall by any means hurt you."[88] Did you notice the allusions to the Garden of Eden? I told you this portion of Adam's legend, is just as full of analogies as the previous chapter.

Genesis 4:16 And Cain went out from the presence of the LORD, and dwelt in the land of Nod, on the east of Eden.

Genesis 4:17 And Cain knew his wife; and she conceived, and bare Enoch: and he builded a city, and called the name of the city, after the name of his son, Enoch.

Genesis 4:18 And unto Enoch was born Irad: and Irad begat Mehujael: and Mehujael begat Methusael: and Methusael begat Lamech.

Immediately, when I look at these verses, my mind questions how can Cain be a wanderer, yet dwell in Nod? The Hebrew word for Nod means, "Wandering." Evidently, they traveled for some years before settling in Nod. Therefore, Cain did not wander forever. Israel could immediately connect with this image, after wandering in the wilderness for forty years. Here we have yet another allusion, this time connecting sin to wandering.

As I said before, Cain prefigures Ishmael. In these verses, we see the lineage of Cain. God blesses him to produce a people or nation from his loins. Notice there is no curse put on his descendants. They can be as close or far from God as they please.

When Adam sinned, they went eastward into Eden. God placing the cherubim at the eastside of the garden alludes to this. After Cain sins, he also heads east to Nod. I would think God kicking them out was the essential point. Why does the writer stress the direction in the narrative?

Direction is important in a purely spiritual sense, as it relates to God. The Sun signifies the Lord in the Bible and it usually symbolizes the most important deities in mythology. From the viewpoint of the Earth, the sun rises in the east and sets in the west. In actuality, the sun neither rises nor sets. This too is a biblical truth.[89] If God does not sleep or slumber, then there is no need for Him to rise.

Since the sun traverses the sky from east to west, this is the proverbial path of God. It therefore becomes important to note the direction of individuals, in relation to the Lord. If we move west, then we are in line with Him. However, if we move east, we are going in the opposite direction. This illustrates our spiritual relationship. Therefore, with Adam and Cain, we see humanity moving further and further from God.

Genesis 4:19 And Lamech took unto him two wives: the name of the one *was* Adah, and the name of the other Zillah.
Genesis 4:20 And Adah bare Jabal: he was the father of such as dwell in tents, and *of such as have* cattle.
Genesis 4:21 And his brother's name *was* Jubal: he was the father of all such as handle the harp and organ.
Genesis 4:22 And Zillah, she also bare Tubalcain, an instructer of every artificer in brass and iron: and the sister of Tubalcain *was* Naamah.
Genesis 4:23 And Lamech said unto his wives, Adah and Zillah, Hear my voice; ye wives of Lamech, hearken unto my speech: for I have slain a man to my wounding, and a young man to my hurt.
Genesis 4:24 If Cain shall be avenged sevenfold, truly Lamech seventy and sevenfold.

The listing of Cain's descendants gives us more historical timelines. "The first named person in the Bible, to have lived in a tent was named Jabal. He was the brother of the ancient Biblical ruler of Euphrates named King Nimrod. King Nimrod created a civilization and defied God by creating the biggest structure in the planet (the tower of Babel). Jabal, however, decided to live a simple life around the desert and thus he was blessed with countless flock. Jabal is considered the grandfather of Hebrew and Bedouin/Arab lifestyle."[90]

Jubal is the father of those who play the harp and organ. "The harp is one of the oldest musical instruments in the world. The earliest harps were developed from the hunting bow. The wall paintings of ancient Egyptian tombs dating from as early as 3000 B.C. show an instrument that closely resembles the hunter's bow, without the pillar that we find in modern harps."[91]

Tubalcain was an instructor in brass and ironwork. "In archaeology, the Iron Age was the stage in the development of any people in which tools and weapons whose main ingredient was iron were prominent. The adoption of this material often coincided with other changes in society, including differing agricultural practices, religious beliefs and artistic styles. In history, the Iron Age is the last principal period in the three-age system for classifying prehistoric societies, preceded by the Bronze Age. Its date and context vary depending on the country or geographical region."[92] Therefore, the purpose of showing Cain's lineage is to take us from the Silver Age to the Iron Age.

At the end of the narrative, Lamech kills a man just like Cain, but he has a reason for his actions. The New International Version of the Bible makes it clearer.

> *Genesis 4:23 Lamech said to his wives, "Adah and Zillah, listen to me; wives of Lamech, hear my words.* ***I have killed a man for wounding me, a young man for injuring me.***
> *Genesis 4:24 If Cain is avenged seven times, then Lamech seventy-seven times."*

Lamech makes an interesting declaration to his wives, he says, "If Cain was avenged sevenfold, then he will be requited seventy-seven times." His reasoning seems to be if Cain kills his own brother without justification and he kills for a cause, then surely God must avenge him even more.

He judges himself better than Cain, this is pride. In his arrogance, Lamech does not see that God's grace is the reason for the protection of Cain. Lamech does not deserve the Lord's grace any more than Cain does. This is the point of grace. The focus is on the goodness of God and not us. Jesus addresses this type of thinking in his parable of the Householder.[93] Without the graciousness of the Lord, we would all perish.

Another thing to note is the writer contrasting the lineages of Cain to Seth. When we view the descendants of Cain, we see their work. However, in Genesis 5, occupations of Seth's offspring are not mentioned, just their long life spans. Their lengthy existences signify they are the sons of God. This is a continuation of the Ishmael, Isaac saga.

Cain's descendants represent the flesh, which is why the writer highlights the work of their hands. Conversely, Seth's lineage illustrates righteousness is by faith, not works.

> *Romans 9:6 Not as though the word of God hath taken none effect.* ***For they are not all Israel, which are of Israel:***
> *Romans 9:7 Neither, because they are the seed of Abraham, are they all children:*** but, In Isaac shall thy seed be called.***
> *Romans 9:8 That is,* ***They which are the children of the flesh, these are not the children of God: but the children of the promise are counted for the seed.***

Romans 9:9 For this is the word of promise, At this time will I come, and Sara shall have a son.
Romans 9:10 And not only this; but when Rebecca also had conceived by one, even by our father Isaac;
*Romans 9:11 **(For the children being not yet born, neither having done any good or evil, that the purpose of God according to election might stand, not of works, but of him that calleth;)***

As Paul said, salvation is a gift of God; it does not come through works.[94] Otherwise, individuals would have a reason to boast. If we could attain salvation through works, it would be sinful, not holy. Remember, sin is anything that goes against our purpose (love). The Bible clearly states, "Love does not boast and is not proud."[95]

Genesis 4:25 And Adam knew his wife again; and she bare a son, and called his name Seth: For God, *said she*, hath appointed me another seed instead of Abel, whom Cain slew.
Genesis 4:26 And to Seth, to him also there was born a son; and he called his name Enos: then began men to call upon the name of the LORD.

The name Seth in the Hebrew language means compensation. We have at the close of the chapter another son to recompense Eve for Abel. God told the city of Eve that her seed would crush the head of the serpent. Abel was the seed God promised her. Therefore, in order to fulfill the promise, a replacement was essential.

The lineage of Seth in chapter five of Genesis, demonstrates God keeping his promise to the Woman. The long lifespans illustrates they are the sons of God. Still, plainly the scripture states Adam, "Had a son in his own likeness, in his own image and he named him Seth." This is a pictorial representation of the fall of humanity.

In verse twenty-six, we find a curious statement. Seth had a son and named him Enos, and then men began to call on the name of the Lord. How could this be the beginning of humans calling or praying to God, when Cain and Abel offered sacrifices to Him?

Remember earlier, I said, we became detached from God this resulted in our spiritual death. We started searching for God outside of ourselves. However, He is within us. We formed religions, rituals and rules, in order to earn the Lord's favor. Thousands of years transpired between Adam and Enos. If we use Cain's, descendants as a historical guide for time. Three generations from Adam, takes us from the Golden Age to the Bronze Period.

As time elapsed, the serpent caused the sons of God to forget the Lord dwelt inside of them. After the birth of Enos humanity has no concept of God being within. Therefore, they begin to call upon the Lord.

Think about it this way, you do not call someone who is with you. If you do, they respond by saying, why are you calling me I am right here. God is not by us, He is in us. You cannot get closer than that. In one sense calling on the Lord, is like calling yourself. All of this is a result of the fall. Thankfully, Jesus has reconciled all things. Now via the Holy Spirit we know God dwells inside of us.

Logically, this should be the end of the narrative. There are a series of covenants ultimately leading us to the true seed, Jesus Christ. However, God does not allow the story to end this way. What is missing from the narrative?

We know what happened to Seth and all his of the descendants. They became the nation of Israel. This nation birthed the promised Messiah, end of the story. Paradoxically, Christ is also the beginning of the story. However, we do not know what became of Cain's descendants, we lost track of them. Why is this important?

We readily identify with Adam and Eve as the literal start of humanity. In the fall, we acknowledge we are included. But, we are like the hypocrite Jesus described in the book of St. Matthew.

> *St. Matthew 7:3* **And why beholdest thou the mote that is in thy brother's eye, but considerest not the beam that is in thine own eye?**
> *St. Matthew 7:4* Or how wilt thou say to thy brother, Let me pull out the mote out of thine eye; and, behold, a beam is in thine own eye?
> *St. Matthew 7:5* **Thou hypocrite, first cast out the beam out of thine own eye; and then shalt thou see clearly to cast out the mote out of thy brother's eye.**

A hypocrite, that is unduly harsh, Jesus' words cannot apply to us. Even the apostle Paul thought Eve (the female) was deceived, but not Adam (the male).[96] This was somehow justification for women not being equal to men. Unfortunately, this ideology became the scriptural basis for centuries of discrimination. This is a clear case of having a beam in our eye. It is self-justification via hypocritical thinking.

Although we somewhat identify with the story of the fall. No one identifies with Cain in the narrative. He transferred his anger at God to his brother. Cain is a murderer and killed his brother without real justification. His sin is in a different category than ours.

Many believe the Bible declares humanity started from one source, the literal Adam and Eve. This means we are all one big family. Even science agreed claiming the DNA of every individual is 99.9% alike.

Therefore, all acts of violence are domestic. Anyone you have ever hated, fought against, lied to, teased or denied helping, is in fact your brother or sister. We only vary from each other by 0.01%. Yet we have devised an innumerable amount of differences between each other, resulting in an, us against them mentality. We cannot see everyone is our brother, because there is a beam in our eye.

In actuality, Adam (male and female) were not the first or only humans on the planet in the Genesis account. "New finding by science agree this view, suggesting humans are closer to 99.5% - 99% alike."[97] If you take the Genesis account literally or not, the point is still the same, we are all related.

What does any of this have to do with Cain and his descendants? Everything, the whole Bible is a story about a father and his two sons. It boils down to God and his offspring. In the Old Testament, it is Israel and the heathen nations. In the New Testament, it is believers and non-believers, also called saints and sinners. It is always just the two. Since Jesus restores all things, how can the story of Cain remain unresolved?

Jesus reveals to us that God has restored Cain. The essence of God is love. If Cain is a son of God, then God must be his father. When Cain killed Abel, he leaves and is never reconciled to his natural father (Adam). Jesus in parable form shows us the true reconciliation. It is the parable of the Prodigal Son.

Notice how the parable starts, "A certain man had two sons."[98] One son left and wandered to a faraway country. The righteous son stayed with the father. Cain symbolizes the son who left, Seth is the son who stayed and God denotes the father. The wanderer comes to himself and returns home. This means, the issue was with the son's mind, his thought process was flawed. The father forgives his sins and restores him. This is grace! Clearly, if we remove the beam from our eye, we can see the truth of this parable and the Bible. We are Cain.

The apostle Paul puts it this way, "What then? Are we better than they? No, in no wise: for we have before proved both Jews and Gentiles, that they are all under sin; As it is written, There is none righteous, no, not one."[99]

Remember, Adam and Cain both headed eastwards from Eden, away from the movement of the sun (God). All God requires of us is repentance, which simply means to turn around.

Robert
Your brother in Christ

References

[1] Vermes, Gaza. The Complete Dead Sea Scroll in English. [Online] <http://www.thechristianidentityforum.net/downloads/Complete-Scrolls.pdf>
[2] Merriam-Webster Online Dictionary. <http://www.merriam-webster.com/dictionary/science>
[3] Hawking, Stephen and Mlodinow, Leonard. The Grand Design. (New York: Bantam Books, 2010) p. 172.
[4] Davis, Robert. 6 Things Every Christian Should Know: The Fundamentals of Christianity. (Connecticut: Kingdom Works Publishing, 2009) p. 27.
[5] Holy Bible. James 2:20.
[6] Davis, Robert. How to Live the Abundant Life. (Connecticut: Kingdom Works Publishing, 2011) p. 95.
[7] Holy Bible, Deuteronomy 4:29.
[8] Science Daily. Quantum Theory Demonstrated: Observation affects Reality. [Online] < http://www.sciencedaily.com/releases/1998/02/980227055013.htm>
[9] Hawking and Mlodinow. The Grand Design. p.180.
[10] Holy Bible. Isaiah 45:22.
[11] Universe 101: Big Bang Theory. [Online] < http://map.gsfc.nasa.gov/universe/bb_theory.html>
[12] Ibid. < http://map.gsfc.nasa.gov/universe/uni_life.html >
[13] Holy Bible. Romans 15:5.
[14] Big Bang: How Did the Universe Begin? Takahashi, Yuki D. Spring 2000 [Online] <http://www.ugcs.caltech.edu/~yukimoon/BigBang/BigBang.htm >
[15] The Archean Eon and the Hadean. [Online] <http://www.ucmp.berkeley.edu/precambrian/archean_hadean.php>
[16] The Proterozoic Eon. [Online] < http://www.ucmp.berkeley.edu/precambrian/proterozoic.php>
[17] The formation of the Moon. [Online] < http://hyperphysics.phy-astr.gsu.edu/hbase/astro/moonhab.html>
[18] Leviathan. < http://en.wikipedia.org/wiki/Leviathan>
[19] The Extinction of Dinosaurs. Milwaukee Public Museum. [Online] <http://www.mpm.edu/collections/pubs/geology/dinoextinct/>

[20] Biodiversity and Conservation: A hypertext Book by Peter J. Bryant. Chapter 3:The Age of Mammals. [Online] < http://darwin.bio.uci.edu/~sustain/bio65/lec03/b65lec03.htm>
[21] Miller, James B. An Evolving Dialogue: Theological and Scientific Perspectives on Evolution. (Pennsylvania, Trinity Press International, 2001) p. 347.
[22] Ibid.
[23] Ibid.
[24] Is Mathematics a Science? Mathematical Proof. [Online] < http://www.arachnoid.com/is_math_a_science/index.html>
[25] Davis, Robert. The Final Message. Understanding the Book of Revelation. (Connecticut: Kingdom Works Publishing, 2008) p. 83
[26] Creationism versus Science. What are the Main Arguments for Evolution? [Online] < http://www.creationtheory.org/Introduction/Page04.xhtml>
[27] Hawking, Stephen and Mlodinow, Leonard. The Grand Design. (New York: Bantam Books, 2010) p. 172.
[28] Ibid., p.180.
[29] CNN Transcripts. CNN Larry King Live. Interview with Stephen Hawking; Science and Religion. Aired September 10, 2010 - 21:00 ET [Online] <http://transcripts.cnn.com/TRANSCRIPTS/1009/10/lkl.01.html>
[30] Ibid.
[31] Ibid.
[32] Evidence for an Ancient Earth. Radiometric Dating – A Christian Perspective. Dr. Roger C. Weins. [Online] < http://www.indiana.edu/~ensiweb/evid.anc.earth.pdf>
[33] Universe 101: Big Bang Theory. [Online] < http://map.gsfc.nasa.gov/universe/bb_theory.html>
[34] Ibid. < http://map.gsfc.nasa.gov/universe/uni_life.html >
[35] The Origin of the Earth's Atmosphere. [Online] <http://atlantic.evsc.virginia.edu/~bph/AW_Book_Spring_96/AW_Book_11.html>
[36] Evolution of the Atmosphere: Composition, Structure and Energy. The Earliest Atmosphere, Oceans and Continents. <http://www.globalchange.umich.edu/globalchange1/current/lectures/Perry_Samson_lectures/evolution_atm/index.html>
[37] The Climate System. Early Earth and the Evolution of the Atmosphere. < http://eesc.columbia.edu/courses/ees/climate/lectures/earth.html>
[38] Earth formation. < http://www.universetoday.com/58177/earth-formation/>

[39] When did oceans form on the Earth? What evidence is preserved in the rock record?
< http://serc.carleton.edu/NAGTWorkshops/earlyearth/questions/formation_oceans.html>
[40] The Restless Earth: A Geologic Primer. The Supercontinent Cycle.
< http://www.burkemuseum.org/static/geo_history_wa/The%20Restless%20Earth%20v.2.0.htm>
[41] Evolution of the Solar System and the Planets. How the planets were formed?
< http://www.globalchange.umich.edu/globalchange1/current/lectures/evolution_star/evolution_star.html>
[42] Ibid. The role of dust grains.
[43] Seasons of the Earth. < http://vnatsci.ltu.edu/s_schneider/astro/wbstla2k/mytalk/seasons.shtml>
[44] Science Now. Who needs a Moon? < http://news.sciencemag.org/sciencenow/2011/05/who-needs-a-moon.html?ref=hp>
[45] Origins of Modern Humans: Multiregional or Out of Africa? Donald Johnson. <http://www.actionbioscience.org/evolution/johanson.html>
[46] Is There Really Scientific Evidence for a Young Earth?
< http://www.lpl.arizona.edu/~matthewt/yeclaimsbeta.html#civ>
[47] Top Ten Myths About Evolution (And One Extra).
< http://www.uwgb.edu/dutchs/pseudosc/top10mythsevol.htm>
[48] Ibid.
[49] God and Evolution. < http://www.talkorigins.org/faqs/faq-god.html>
[50] Ibid.
[51] 15 Answers to Creationist Nonsense. < http://www.ksu.edu/biology/pob/sciam2002.pdf>
[52] Christian Teaching Resources. Does Evolution Disprove God? Are Science and Religion Compatible?
< http://www.christianteaching.org.uk/doesevolutiondisprovegod.html>
[53] Universal Myths and Symbols: Animal Creatures and Creation.
< http://www.yale.edu/ynhti/curriculum/units/1998/2/98.02.05.x.html>
[54] The Hebrew Creation Narrative (Genesis 1-3).
<http://public.wsu.edu/~brians/world_civ/worldcivreader/world_civ_reader_1/hebrew_creation.html>
[55] Ibid.
[56] Allegory. [Online] <https://en.wikipedia.org/wiki/Allegory>

[57] Howe, Richard G PhD. Rethinking Adam in the Garden. < http://www.richardghowe.com/Adam.pdf>
[58] Ibid.
[59] Ibid.
[60] Studdert-Kennedy, Michael. Language Development from an Evolutionary Perspective. <http://www.haskins.yale.edu/sr/SR101/SR101_02.pdf>
[61] The Adam and Eve Story: Eve Came From Where? The Biblical Archeology Society. January 2, 2017, https://www.biblicalarchaeology.org/daily/biblical-topics/bible-interpretation/the-adam-and-eve-story-eve-came-from-where/
[62] Holy Bible. Galatians 4:25-26.
[63] Fields, Chris. Why do we talk to ourselves? < http://www.mendeley.com/catalog/we-talk-ourselves/#page-1>
[64] Holy Bible. Romans 5:13.
[65] The Franklin Institute Online. The Human Brain. <http://www.fi.edu/learn/brain/fats.html>
[66] Stanford, Craig B. The Hunting Apes: Meat Eating and the Origins of Human Behavior. < http://press.princeton.edu/titles/6549.html>
[67] Holy Bible. Genesis 3:7.
[68] Holy Bible. St. Luke 7:34.
[69] Human Evolution. <http://en.wikipedia.org/wiki/Human_evolution>
[70] Holy Bible. St. Luke 17:20-21.
[71] Holy Bible. Romans 10:17.
[72] Davis. How to Live the Abundant Life. p. 43-45.
[73] Holy Bible. Philippians 4:13.
[74] Holy Bible. Job 14:1.
[75] Holy Bible. Genesis 6:3.
[76] Holy Bible. Proverbs 23:7.
[77] Holy Bible. Revelation 21:18-20.
[78] Holy Bible. 1 Kings 5:1-12.
[79] Holy Bible. Psalms 2:7-9.
[80] Holy Bible. Hebrews 4:15.
[81] Holy Bible. Philippians 2:5.
[82] Holy Bible. St. Matthew 7:6.
[83] Holy Bible. St. Luke 22:31.
[84] The Coming of Farming. < http://www.timemaps.com/farming>
[85] Slate. What was the original domesticated animal? <http://www.slate.com/articles/news_and_politics/explainer/2009/03/mans_first_friend.html>
[86] Ages of Man. < http://en.wikipedia.org/wiki/Ages_of_Man>

[87] Holy Bible. Psalms 103:10.
[88] Holy Bible. St. Luke 10:18-19.
[89] Holy Bible. Psalms 121:4.
[90] Tents in History. < http://tentsnstuff.com/tents-in-history/>.
[91] The International Harp Museum. History of the Harp.
< http://www.internationalharpmuseum.org/visit/history.html>.
[92] Ancient Encyclopedia History. Iron Age. < http://www.ancient.eu.com/Iron_Age/>
[93] Holy Bible. St. Matthew 20:1-16.
[94] Holy Bible. Ephesians 2:8-9.
[95] Holy Bible. 1 Corinthians 13:4.
[96] Holy Bible. 1 Timothy 2:11-15.
[97] Study: Humans' DNA Not Quite So Similar. <http://www.redorbit.com/news/science/1054012/study_humans_dna_not_quite_so_similar/>.
[98] Holy Bible. St. Luke 15:11-32.
[99] Holy Bible. Romans 3:9-10.

www.ingramcontent.com/pod-product-compliance
Lightning Source LLC
LaVergne TN
LVHW051058080426
835508LV00019B/1951